THE NONPROFIT PLAYBOOK

THE ESSENTIAL 12 STEP GUIDE TO SUSTAINABLE SUCCESS

ELIZABETH V. MARING

RIVERAUTHOR
PRESS

ISBN 978-1-7353584-0-6   (Paperback)
ISBN 978-1-7353584-1-3   (ebook)

For my generous, discerning, and loving husband, Clarence.

Download The Companion Workbook for FREE!

READ THIS FIRST

Just to say thanks for buying my book, I would like to give you the companion workbook for FREE!

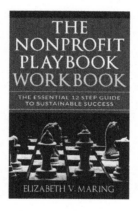

TO DOWNLOAD THE FREE WORKBOOK, GO TO:

https://elizabethmaring.com

TABLE OF CONTENTS

INTRODUCTION

"I have no power to control the weather,
but I can bring an umbrella."

A good friend of mine recently bought a new car. It has a lot of bells and whistles: auto-emergency braking, lane departure signals, and a blind spot warning system. He's connected to emergency services through an inside SOS button, and he can rely on receiving forward collision warnings. His engine performance is constantly monitored, and messages will appear on his dash if there's the slightest malfunction. The car can even take control of itself to prevent a crash! The instruction manual is three inches thick. Here's what we know for sure: many car professionals have worked very hard for a very long time to keep my friend safe against the hazards of driving on today's roadways. What a gift.

If only I had had the equivalent of a smart car manual when I started serving in nonprofit leadership roles thirty-five years ago. What I wouldn't have given for a roadmap of the ins and outs of the most common nonprofit problems and solid guidance about how to start resolving them. It would have saved me—and the nonprofits I served—so much time and money. What if you, as a nonprofit leader, were given ways *today* to detect and protect your charitable organization from the most predictable top twelve threats to sustainability *before* the resulting bad newspaper headlines, reputational damage, loss of staff and drop in donor support? What if you were given ways to build sustainability through effective fundraising, an enduring mission, successful conflict management, and a brilliant succession plan?

This is exactly why I wrote this book. I want to give nonprofit leaders a handy resource *packed* with easy-to-understand nuggets of wisdom to use as they navigate their various leadership roles. I want this book to be a utility tool for boards and staff leaders that will prove helpful over and over again. I hope this book starts important team conversations about the challenges common to all nonprofits in one season or another. Most importantly, I want to share valuable and viable solutions to each of the threats to sustainability presented in this book.

My experience has come from serving continuously on nonprofit boards with annual budgets ranging from $100,000 to $270 million. As an attorney, I have represented for-profit and nonprofit clients for over 30 years. In 2011, I became a nonprofit president and executive director when I founded a 25,000-square-foot charitable resale store in Arlington Heights, Illinois that to date has spun off nearly three million dollars in grants and goods for educational scholarships and homeless intervention. Nonprofit service is my passion. I have been at the table as a leader, as a lawyer, and as a volunteer. Throughout the years and in many circumstances, I have seen nonprofits at their best and at their worst.

Let's look at some surprising facts about nonprofits. According to the National Center for Charitable Statistics (NCCS) and the National Council of Nonprofits, in 2015 more than 1.56 million nonprofit organizations were registered in the United States. They employ over 11.4 million people, or just over 10% of the American workforce. This number includes public nonprofits, private foundations, and other types of nonprofit organizations, including local chambers of commerce, fraternal organizations, and civic leagues. The economic and societal impact of nonprofits is huge, both domestically and globally. In 2015, nonprofits contributed $985.4 billion dollars to the US economy, or 5.4% of the national GDP. These figures represent 8.7 billion hours of volunteer labor and energy expended for the common good.[1]

But nearly 66% of all nonprofits operate on a budget of under $500,000 per year! Only 14.6% have budgets of one to five million, and only 5.3% have budgets over ten million.[2]. In the United States, charitable work is done mainly by small groups of townspeople working together to solve local community problems. As a result, these communities enjoy greater direct benefit from—and exercise more local control over—these nonprofit organizations. Nonprofits truly are friends working together.

Whether you're reading this book as a founder, an executive director, board member, staff leader, or someone just entering nonprofit service, every nonprofit—including yours—is too important to be lost to avoidable mistakes and mismanagement. Please don't fall into the trap of thinking that these challenges could never happen to your nonprofit. Many of them are directly in your path. There's something in this book to benefit every nonprofit organization now or later.

My encouragement to you is this: Go ahead and skip to the chapter that is the most helpful to your immediate interest or problem, and then go back and extract the gold in each chapter to ensure the sustainable success of your nonprofit. Sustainable success depends both on doing the right things and not doing the wrong ones. This book will closely examine a number of nonprofit successes and failures through case studies and reveal the lessons that you can apply today. For the sake of your own leadership, staff, volunteers, donors, and clients, I hope you'll read the entire book.

CHAPTER 1

STEP 1: TAKE CONTROL OF THE MONEY PROBLEM

> *"If you make meaning, you'll make money."*
>
> — Guy Kawasaki

The top twelve reasons why your nonprofit doesn't have enough money

There are few things more stressful to nonprofit leaders than chronic anxiety about whether an organization will be able to keep its doors open. No single problem in nonprofit world drives leaders into crisis mode faster than discovering an immediate, significant, and surprise budget shortfall. A lack of cash flow threatens a nonprofit's ability to fulfill its missional promises. What's that familiar axiom? No money, no mission?

I clearly remember the night about ten years ago arriving home very late and waking my husband. I had just attended my first board meeting of Do Good, Inc.[3] and said, "I think Do Good has less than a 50/50 chance of avoiding bankruptcy. Its finances are a disaster." From the outside, Do Good looked successful, but from the inside, the financial picture was in shambles. Creditor payments were way behind. Truthfully, I thought about immediately resigning from the board, but the cause was compelling, and I'm weirdly attracted to train wrecks. Thankfully, Do Good did avoid bankruptcy and is doing fine today. But it was a long, hard process for all involved.

Here's where the recovery started. The first steps to permanently solving a chronic lack of operating funds is facing reality and deeply understanding the causes for it at a data-driven level. Acting to solve a money problem without first understanding the underlying reasons for the shortfall increases the chances that it will happen over and over again.

There are many reasons why nonprofits run out of money, but here are twelve common ones to help you get started:

1. The nonprofit donor support base is too small. The organization either relies heavily on a few large donors, or government funding that unexpectedly decreases or stops.

2. The nonprofit poorly manages existing income and assets. Good financial policies and controls are missing.

3. The nonprofit's marketing is inadequate, resulting in low brand recognition.

4. The nonprofit fails to communicate with donors in a regular and compelling way about mission achievements and needs.

5. The nonprofit expanded past the amount of available funding to support more growth. Zeal for the cause pushed past realistic financial projections and limits.

6. A large financial bet was placed on a failed initiative.

7. The board did not plan for a rainy day, and the organization lacked emergency or contingency funds essential in a downturn.

8. The nonprofit is a victim of embezzlement, fraud, or other malfeasance.

9. One of the nonprofit's income-producing services or products has stopped producing revenue.

10. The nonprofit has flawed fundraising efforts because it is often hard for small, cash-strapped nonprofits to fund the skills, experience, best practices, tracking, and accountability needed for successful fundraising.

11. Good fundraising campaigns have fallen short of goals, or donors have not fulfilled pledges.

12. Nonprofit leadership has failed to understand and monitor both the nonprofit's revenue and expenditures closely enough in real time. Put another way, leaders have failed to review what money is coming in and what money is going

out often enough to know if the nonprofit's basic economic model is working.

While the rare nonprofit fails due to a fire or flood, most shortfalls are created by either executive and board mismanagement or unproductive activity. The most important first step is to pinpoint the reasons why your organization is in trouble so you can choose the right remedies and take the right actions.

Nail down why money is so scarce

Financial problems generally have underlying causes with deeper roots. An empty checkbook creates an instant desire to fling open the doors and shout a panicked plea to supporters for financial help. But taking some time to understand the underlying causes of the shortfall will help you craft better money-generating solutions, give you a fuller story to tell your donors, and provide greater assurance that the money you raise won't be thrown into a bucket with a hole in it.

Practically speaking, you may also have only one last bite at your donor apple, so it makes sense not to waste it. Even your most committed donors will want to know what you did with their last crisis donation. They will take note if your nonprofit is always going from one financial predicament to another.

Case Study #1: How one nonprofit came back from the brink

Here is how one large church in the United States got into financial trouble but was able to restore its financial health. The church owned seventy-seven acres on the side of town that was growing, but sold it to purchase a failing mall in a declining part of town. The mall was almost completely empty of tenants, but the church wanted to provide support to nearby city residents by reclaiming the retail space, creating jobs, and providing spiritual support. The purchase exemplified the church's mission, and I admired that it was walking the talk. So, I agreed to join a team to help bring new businesses and services into the mall.

However, crunch time came when the cost of building materials went up and donor pledge payments fell short. The church found itself alarmingly and unexpectedly overextended with its creditors. In response, leadership immediately formed a task force to study the problems and propose solutions, scaled back renovation plans, and negotiated favorable repayment schedules with creditors.

I was asked to work as a consultant with a team tasked with finding creative ways to fill mall space not being used for church activities. That was when I began earnestly tuning in to my mother-in-law's chatter about a very successful thrift store in Kalamazoo, Michigan. She had volunteered there for years, and the profit numbers she was quoting really got my attention. I wondered whether that concept could be adapted to the new church property. After some careful planning, the church wound up converting thirty thousand square feet of empty mall space into two complementary thrift stores. Within two years, the stores produced nearly a million dollars in income for the church by using volunteer labor and selling donated goods. The stores also paid the church market-rate rent! Win-win-win.

The neighborhood benefited from the availability of gently used goods at discounted prices, too. Eventually the church recovered financially and reputationally. It is thriving today. Unknown to me at the time, that experience would prepare me to start the Community Threads resale store several years later to benefit the homeless population in northern Illinois.

There are so many great lessons in this church story. When financial problems hit, the church's first act was to unleash a joint board and staff task force to find the underlying reasons why, when more people were attending and overall giving was up, the church was stumbling financially. They discovered that, in the years leading up to the mall purchase, they had failed to build sufficient internal infrastructure to support the church's rapid growth. The missing system support needed for such a huge project led to the board making spending decisions with insufficient facts.

Once the financial crisis came to light, they instituted stricter churchwide budgetary controls that had been more relaxed when resources were plentiful. What had been passable financial management in the early stages of the church developed into robust financial management for the long haul. In short, they started to count their pennies as well as their dollars. The church found ways to instill accountability in every area, so the potential for another financial surprise became remote while they continued to maintain high interpersonal trust with staff, congregants, creditors, and donors.

From the onset of the crisis, leadership committed itself to being transparent with the congregation and creditors about the failures and fixes. They regularly held public meetings to discuss progress and setbacks as they happened. By guarding those important donor, creditor, and member relationships with action, honesty, and updates, the leaders preserved the church's future and promoted a quicker recovery.

If your nonprofit is in a tough financial spot, take heart. Coming up next are suggestions to strengthen your organization's financial health. Embrace the truth about root causes, even if they are disappointing and painful. Push away denial and wishful thinking. Reality is always a friend. The more certainty you have about *why* your organization is suffering, the greater your chances of finding the best, quickest, and most permanent ways out.

Six ways to bring financial health back to your nonprofit

1. Stop digging a bigger hole

Once you've uncovered the root causes of the red ink, explore fixes inside and outside your organization. First, consider cutting costs;

you have immediate control over these, and they can usually be cut more quickly than you can ramp up outside fundraising. The hard part is knowing *what* to cut. Keep in mind, too, that it's hard to cut your way to success. Fundraising must be done soon after cost-cutting, so be sure not to get stuck in this process for too long.

Denis Winston Healy, Britain's Secretary of Defense from 1964 to 1970, famously created the First Law of Holes, which states, "When in one, stop digging." Why? Because digging a hole deeper makes it harder to get out! The humor of the saying is in its obviousness, but actually doing it can be harder than you might think. Spending patterns and attitudes inside organizations often resist change and tighter controls.

Sometimes dire circumstances necessitate cuts in expenses that go beyond reducing perks and "non-essentials." Layoffs and benefit reductions are, sadly, sometimes unavoidable. Of course, it's wise to do all you can to protect people and what matters most to them. But if the life of the nonprofit is at stake, leaders must keep the nonprofit's mission foremost in mind. Wisdom dictates that all options be put on the table for consideration in order to pull the nonprofit out of financial distress.

2. Avoid creating the doom loop

Leaders of a nonprofit in financial trouble should avoid the doom loop while cutting expenses. A doom loop happens if too many of the nonprofit's revenue-generating activities are reduced while in crisis mode, thereby orchestrating its own long-term demise. Consequently, when cutting expenses related to human resources, income production, or fundraising, determine how those cuts will impact future revenue. For example, layoffs in the marketing and development offices are usually made last.

Cost reductions start by targeting fat or bloat. Common examples of expendable perks include providing food at organizational gatherings, limiting credit card privileges, and halting all non-essential travel for staff. Additional cost savings include hiring freezes and offering early retirement packages to those who desire it.

Most nonprofits cut jobs as a last, painful measure. Protect morale by taking care to explain the reasons behind the reduction in force, as well as why the reduction process is fair. When reducing staff positions, use objective criteria that demonstrate fairness by applying them across the board; this will help keep the nonprofit away from claims of wrongful termination. Always consult human resource experts and legal counsel when reducing staff. Some nonprofits choose to provide out-placement services to help released employees find and transition to new jobs. Communicate clearly and compassionately but don't sugar coat the truth which often leads to people feeling misled later.

3. Model financial sacrifice

Another positive course of action I've seen leaders take to preserve morale is making a personal financial sacrifice on behalf of the nonprofit. This might mean taking a voluntary pay cut, or reducing your own benefits. By putting "skin in the game" and betting on the nonprofit's recovery, you can inspire and encourage others to do the same. In the case study above, my consulting business forgave over $20,000 in fees to help the church's recovery. Other vendors likewise agreed to longer repayment plans or reduced balances.

I've watched the leadership team of a $270-million nonprofit roll back their salaries to the previous year's level to show responsibility-taking and leadership when the nonprofit hit a financial iceberg on their watch. Of course, not every leader can afford to do something like this, and that's OK. But if it is possible for the board, staff leaders, or friends of the nonprofit to make even a temporary sacrifice, it can be very inspiring to others who bear the biggest brunt of the belt-tightening.

Finally, whenever possible, increase credibility by tangibly demonstrating your commitment to the cause *before asking outsiders for help*. Often, grant-making organizations will stipulate that financial support from a requesting board must reach 100% participation before a grant request will be considered. It's persuasive to be able to tell donors that all board members are also donors. This is not unreasonable; why should an outside funding source care more about funding your organization than your own board?

Recent Statistics on Board Giving

LAPA Fundraising provides the following stats on board giving:[4]

- In multiple studies, fundraising ranks #1 among board areas needing improvement. Only 5% of charities listed fundraising as a board strength.

- Only 46% of boards have all members giving.

- Overall, boards average 74% in member giving.

- 68% of nonprofits required their board members to make annual personal donations. Of those, 40% suggested a minimum annual donation of $150 per year. However, the best practice is $1,000 a year.

- Boards requiring donor identification from members: 61%.

- Boards requiring attendance at fundraising events from members: 60%.

4. Consider exploring new revenue sources while avoiding unrelated business income tax (UBIT)

Some nonprofits can develop products and services that will create new sources of related income.

Perhaps your organization could produce a book or training materials for distribution online. Maybe new technology can help you deliver core services more effectively for less cost. If your nonprofit owns real estate, can it be sold, and the proceeds used to fuel an area that is showing greater growth? If the nonprofit is a conferencing organization, is there a way to offer online alternatives using existing materials?

In all cases, make sure to do two things:

- Have all potential revenue streams reviewed by qualified professionals with legal and accounting backgrounds to avoid incurring unrelated business income tax (UBIT). This advice will prevent the possible loss of your charitable status with the IRS, and keep the nonprofit well within the legal parameters of permissible nonprofit activity.

- Weed out overly idealistic, desperate, poorly modeled, distracting efforts that actually end up costing your nonprofit money.

5. Utilize new products and services

For nonprofit colleges and universities, the financial sector is developing new tools to help colleges and universities assess the return on investment of course offerings so that boards and administrators can better evaluate which courses attract students and boost revenue. Some nonprofits produce publications and sell ad space. While there may not be money to invest in speculative ventures, there may still be some additional value in existing assets.

Here are a few more questions to ask about income generation.

- Can you collect or increase dues or fees for your organizational programs?

- Is there a way to encourage more paying membership?

- Are there complementary organizations with whom you can collaborate to share facilities, IT expenses, marketing, or create a combined donor pool?

6. Do fundraise, but be smart about it

The need for outside remedies depends on how well the inside remedies have worked to solve your financial problem. As you cut costs, fundraise internally, and develop new potential income streams, also examine outside remedies. Traditional fundraising wisdom holds that the most effective fundraising begins with a compelling story. What is your nonprofit's compelling story? Do you have real data to back up stories of help and hope? Some nonprofits make the mistake of telling donors about financial problems before explaining why the donor should care.

When deciding what to say to donors about your nonprofit, revisit the compelling story that drew you to the nonprofit's mission. Trust that what drew you to the mission will also draw donors and enable them to care about its future. For example, many great hospitals showcase stories of relatable people who have survived serious illness in order to help donors associate their donation with their own potential need for great future medical care.

Transmedia storytelling

For most nonprofits, time and money are precious commodities. Nonetheless, nonprofits should try to engage in transmedia storytelling whenever possible. What is transmedia storytelling? It's a fancy way of saying that your nonprofit story will have greater impact if told across multiple media platforms that link a single story together using current digital technologies. The concept was introduced by Henry Jenkins, a communications professor at USC.

One example of successful transmedia storytelling per Echostories.com is PBS Kids Entertainment.[5] PBS Kids reaches kids not only through television programs, but also through web-based games, learning tools, parental resources, and a mobile app, to name just a few platforms. Nonprofits can also use online tools, interactive websites, mobile apps, and other digital ways to connect to supporters. The key is to tell one compelling story creatively using multiple media technologies.

Remember: dollars follow success

The simple truth is that people root for underdogs but follow winners. It's much more persuasive to capture a story of success and tell donors that a new contribution will enable even more success than telling them that their donation will reverse a financial mess. It will also satisfy their desire to know that their donation is going to a competent agent of real change. If the nonprofit is not being effective in its mission, *that* problem needs to be solved before making any honest appeals for cash.

In the past, nonprofits often sent direct appeal fundraising letters filled with redlined sentences about impending disaster if a donation wasn't received immediately. This was aimed at leveraging a donor's fear. Today's fundraising more often focuses on the good work being done, and what is possible in the future with more donor support. This focus on hope rather than fear is far more effective.

For a long time, nonprofits believed that if donors simply knew about the need, they would donate. While this may still be true for some donors, a better approach to fundraising explains the need, but also explains *how your organization is the most trustworthy source of remedies for that need.* By demonstrating success against a problem, your nonprofit can say, "If you give us funding, we can accomplish even more." Of course, this puts pressure on the nonprofit to produce and prove results. But, in my view, that is a good thing.

First give to donors, then receive

Many donors appreciate help in figuring out the wisest way to be philanthropic. Step into the donor's shoes and figure out what matters to them. Many times, donors wish to see progress against a persistent problem. Sometimes donors want to help a cause that has impacted their own lives. Sometimes they want to fund innovation. By being careful to understand an individual donor's interest and appealing genuinely to it, a nonprofit can reduce the number of false starts in fundraising.

In many cases, an internet search will tell you the causes a donor has previously supported. Fundraising today requires a high degree of emotional intelligence toward the audience. When nonprofits solicit, donors have high expectations of those organizations. This is only becoming more true with an increase in donor-advised fund products. More on that below.

It's important to honor your donor's time and invite them into your story in a way that fits into their preferred delivery system. Most donors no longer enjoy long presentations accompanied by an average dinner. Excellent video productions online, short personal calls or visits, a site tour, and offering potential board service or meaningful volunteer opportunities add interest and a personal touch. Educational trips are a favorite way to increase donor contact.

You'll be rewarded for showing respect for your donor's time, intelligence, and desires of the heart. Some ways to better understand your donors are short surveys or questionnaires. Personal conversations are always the gold standard, but it may be hard to get one-on-one time with busy donors. Sending a solid fundraising letter to all of your donors will help keep your cause in mind. The best fundraisers are those who are genuinely interested in making the wishes and dreams of their donors come true. Donors should be treated as long-term friends.

One of the best things about serving continuously on nonprofit boards over the last thirty years are the amazing moments of stunning generosity I've been privileged to witness. One memory forever etched in my mind was witnessing a generous land developer transfer eighteen million dollars' worth of prime real estate to a nonprofit operating next door to his home. The developer was not connected to the organization other than being its neighbor.

While signing the legal transfer documents, he explained how one of the nonprofit's staff members had taken special care to look in on his family when the developer was hospitalized for cancer treatment. He was extremely impressed by the staff member's thoughtfulness. Mind you, the staff member had no way of knowing that this act of kindness would lead to such a significant gift. Nor was it the reason for his kindness. He was just being a good neighbor.

Here is another story close to my heart. My father was a guy who thought out of the box. He was asked by a local college to fund a scholarship that would bear his name. He agreed, on the condition that he could set the award criteria.

Growing up in a large immigrant family, he had to work in the family hardware store after school and on weekends. Consequently, his grades suffered because he had so little time outside of school and work to do his homework. Before volunteering for the army in WWII he was admitted into college, but only because his church membership meant that the denominational college could not turn him away. My dad was a smart man; he served as a forward observer in the infantry because he was good at math. But he was embarrassed by his academic record.

After the war he created several successful businesses, but he always wished he had earned a college degree and insisted that his five children do so. He decided that the Vogelzang Scholarship should go not to a student with the best grades, but to a student who had faced and overcome the most adversity. Over the years we have heard amazing stories of "Vogelzang Scholars" who have persevered through serious personal setbacks.

Seek out public and corporate funding sources

While private funding contributes heavily to nonprofit revenue, the internet has made online access to public and private grants and foundations more accessible. Whether you choose to work with an organization that specializes in grant writing or to hire staff to develop those connections, your nonprofit mission may be a good fit for specific private or public grants. Investing in a search for those funding sources makes sense.

Nonprofits also find support in the corporate sector. Companies like Allstate Insurance and The Icee Company financially support nonprofits in a variety of ways, including sponsoring employee volunteerism. Starbucks has a program that pays its workers for time spent volunteering at approved nonprofits. Corporate foundations also provide valuable training services and courses for nonprofit employees at a low or reasonable cost. There is more cooperation between the private and the public sectors than ever before.

Convey meaningful gratitude

Lastly, thanking your donors in meaningful ways is the right thing to do, and breeds loyalty. Most donors understand that nonprofits cannot spend lavishly to thank them, nor do they want them to do so. But a personal handwritten note of thanks—rather than a scribbled, "Hey, thanks Joe!" in blue pen at the end of the form fundraising letter or donation receipt—will mean more to a donor.

Make sure handwritten notes are accurate and up to date. They should not say, "Dear John and Mary" if John is deceased. Do not include last year's donation amount in this year's thank you note. Use and spell the donor's name correctly.

My husband's name is Clarence. We have received a number of thank you letters from nonprofits we have supported addressed to "Charles" and "Clearance." I joke with him about bigamy and getting a great deal, but he just rolls his eyes. It's better to have a reminder system in the file to mark significant changes in donor information.

I recently attended a presentation by an investment firm on the exponential growth of *donor-advised funds* (DAF). Donor-advised funds are booming, and they're not without controversy. Here's what *The Chronicle of Philanthropy* says about them: "A donor-advised fund is a little like a personal charitable savings account. A donor creates an account and makes a contribution of cash, stock, or other assets like real estate or artwork and takes an immediate tax deduction for the gift."[6]

The accounts are controlled by a financial nonprofit, such as the nonprofit arm of Vanguard Charitable and Schwab Charitable. These nonprofits invest the assets and manage the donor's account. Once a fund is established, donors tell the sponsoring organization which nonprofits they'd like to donate to from their accounts. Family members of donors are increasingly becoming involved in the selection of recipients, so getting to know a donor's family, if possible, may be very important.

The presenter mentioned above worked for a nonprofit like Schwab Charitable and mentioned that he often receives thank you letters at his office from nonprofit recipients. Since the donation checks come from the entity and not directly from the donor, nonprofits sometimes no longer have direct access to donor addresses. This presenter explained that he passes the thank you letters on to donors, but intentionally highlights those with spelling errors and other signs of carelessness so that the donor will be made aware. Notes of thanks can certainly be simple and heartfelt, but they can never be sloppy.

Summary of Core Points

- Understand the causes for your financial shortfall at a deep and data-driven level in order to permanently stop a chronic money problem.

- Stop all non-essential spending and quickly develop an initial turnaround plan. Update the plan as the evolving financial picture changes, and communicate progress honestly with your stakeholders.

- Avoid creating a doom loop with too many cuts to essential, revenue-generating activities.

- Cut jobs last and protect morale with good communication and fair staff-reduction policies and processes.

- Consult HR and legal professionals when considering eliminating jobs to avoid wrongful termination claims.

- Whenever possible, leadership should model financial support and sacrifice.

- Explore new products and services that do not trigger unrelated business income with the IRS.

- Fundraise through a compelling vision combined with data to prove that progress is being made against the target problem. Showcase how future donations will result in more success.

- Respect your donor's time, intelligence, and desires of the heart before, during, and after your request for money. Thank donors in ways that are meaningful to *them*.

- Investigate additional sources of support in the private and governmental sectors.

- Learn more about the growing field of donor-advised funds.

Coming Up Next

In the next chapter, we'll address the threat to sustainable success of leadership incompetence and misconduct. Every nonprofit deserves emotionally mature, high-integrity, collaborative, effective, courageous, and fiscally responsible leadership. But what if one or more of those attributes is absent in your executive director, president, or CEO? What if this person is not only not leading well, but leading the nonprofit down a harmful or illegal path? What should or can be done?

We hope that all nonprofit leaders are smart, talented, dedicated, and ethical. But chances are you'll meet at least one senior leader over the course of your nonprofit service who needs either good advice, gentle correction, or a boot out the door. Since that boot just might be on your foot, read on to discover how to spot problem leaders early and how to protect your nonprofit from leader misconduct.

CHAPTER 2

STEP 2: SET HIGH
LEADERSHIP STANDARDS

*"You don't lead by hitting people over the head—
that's assault, not leadership."*

— President Dwight D. Eisenhower

There are few things better than working with a leader who presents a compelling vision, develops passionate followers, pursues honorable achievements, instills moral and fiscal integrity, and strives for replicable results. Thankfully, most of us can name at least one executive director, CEO, teacher, pastor, or parent whose leadership shaped our lives in a positive way. Good leaders know how to find the talent in others and elevate it. They empower people and breathe life into great ideas.

However, there are also incompetent and misbehaving leaders who fail the people around them and hinder the mission of an organization meant to do good. Problem leaders can really make a mess of things organizationally, and sometimes hurt their followers, too. *Why* some leaders are flawed is not the subject of this chapter. I'll leave that to the experts in the field of psychology. This chapter is designed to help you flag those behaviors that mark problematic leadership and proposes preventative and remedial solutions if you do.

Five common types of problem nonprofit leaders

1. The incompetent leader

Think for a moment about a time when you saw someone in a leadership position who did not have the right abilities for the job. Unfortunately, people arrive in leadership positions for a lot of reasons besides being competent leaders. Organizations can mistake passion for the cause or other organizational proficiencies for leadership. Other times, nonprofits have a hard time finding leaders of proven ability and settle for someone who's available and really wants the job. Sometimes internal systems work to promote people beyond their ability.

Ironically, leading a nonprofit often requires more leadership talent than leading a for-profit venture. Nonprofit leaders must lead well through influence and persuasion, as well as through position and payroll. Nonprofit leaders often lead volunteers and donors, which requires different skills from leading a paid labor force. They are also nearly always asked to get more done with fewer resources.

Here are three important tests of leadership:

- Can the leader cast a compelling vision?

- Can the leader motivate and direct others to act toward achieving a common goal?

- Can the leader find the resources necessary to succeed?

Those holding a leadership position who are unable to competently do these basic leadership functions create hardship for a nonprofit in the same way a garden suffers without proper doses of sun and rain. One leader friend of mine put it this way, "People complain about leaders who move too fast, but it's a lot harder to push one uphill."

2. The narcissistic leader

Narcissistic leadership can be identified by the degree of energy and focus placed on personal loyalty to the leader rather than on the organization's mission. Usually they tell followers that personal loyalty to them is the same thing as personal loyalty to the organizational mission. Narcissistic leaders can be counted on to make everything about themselves. They can also be very compelling people. They are *just so sure of themselves.*

A narcissistic leadership culture is characterized by followers prioritizing the attention and approval of the leader over producing results for the organization. Staff often feel pressured to agree with the primary leader's opinion and fear repercussions for voicing a contrary one. Narcissistic cultures run on fear and drain energy from the people who work in them.

Feelings of shame and blame are common in followers, even if those feelings are not openly expressed. Narcissistic cultures spend a lot of time burnishing and controlling their primary leader's image. If the narcissism is not countered, an organization can become dependent on this type of leader because everyone becomes trained to wait for his or her opinion. A narcissistic leader's self-focused behavior can easily become normative, accepted, and reinforced by complicit followers.

3. The abusive or harassing leader

All leaders are entrusted with a certain measure of power and authority over people and policies. It's part of the job. But power is also known to be a highly corrupting influence. It's a deep betrayal of trust when the power that comes with leadership is used to control, abuse, and harass others.

Abuse and harassment are identified by instances when the person holding the power insults, bullies, harasses, or takes advantage of the power position in an inappropriate way. Rather than using the power to build people up, abusive leaders tear people down and strip them of some essential choice or right.

Surprisingly, it's not always easy to diagnose and counter abusive leadership. When it's paired with personal or organizational success, those who resist or complain are more easily ignored or intimidated. Of course, as an example, the #MeToo movement highlighted not only the frequency of sexual harassment in the workplace but also the challenges of bringing it to light.

4. The unethical leader

Because public trust is the coin of the realm for all organizations, charitable or not, leaders must model personal integrity. Unethical nonprofit leaders gamble with a nonprofit's public credibility, alienate employees, or lead them to think bad behavior is ok. If left unchecked, unethical leadership usually leads to scandal, financial loss, and sometimes jail time. Sadly, an increase in dishonest leadership in the public square has led to a decline in public trust in leadership in general. This is a serious threat for nonprofits as well.

National Public Radio reported in May 2019 that PwC, one of the nation's largest auditing firms, conducted a study which found that 39% of the 89 CEOs who departed in 2018 left for reasons related to unethical behavior stemming from allegations of sexual misconduct or ethical lapses like fraud, bribery, and insider trading.[7]

Additionally, Dan Prontefract reported on a Deloitte study in *Forbes* magazine that in 2018, 75% of millennials and Gen Z believed leaders and businesses focused on their own agendas rather than considering the wider society, while 62% thought leaders and businesses had no ambition beyond making money. This represents a massive drop in positive public opinion in one year, per *Forbes*.[8] These facts should concern all leaders and prompt greater ethical vigilance.

5. The leader who promotes irresponsibly

Every leader must be able to effectively promote a cause. But the leader who promotes irresponsibly can be identified by the inability to bring a vision to life in a sustainable way. Irresponsible promotion consists of an abundance of compelling visions, personal charm, and exceptional salesmanship that is not equally matched by a sense of duty and commitment to deliver on what is promised in accountable and transparent ways. Defined another way: it is the circuses without the bread. This type of leader typically resists effective oversight and can become belligerent when challenged or restricted.

An irresponsible promoter easily slides between being a charmer, a bully, and a victim—whatever it takes to get their way. They can be unrealistic or reserved about what their plans will really cost, or overly optimistic about how long a project will take to complete. They make followers believe that only big and bold moves will do, and that funding is sure to follow the razzle dazzle. They act quickly without enough planning and run ahead of solid strategic planning developed by a team with reliable data. Naysayers are often maligned as lacking faith or vision.

Special problems associated with founders

Nonprofit founders are a distinctive category of nonprofit leader. They are the people who take an idea for a nonprofit and make it a reality. Most nonprofits owe a deep debt of gratitude to their organizational founders for doing the tremendously hard work of bringing a vision to life. Committed and effective founders break new ground and create many enduring organizations.

But sometimes, founders can fall into the trap of linking their personal interests with the interests of the nonprofit in inappropriate or illegal ways. When founder misconduct *is* discovered, people usually ask why the founder had so much control, why there was not more effective board oversight, and why it took so long for the misconduct to be uncovered. The answers to these questions are often case-specific, but there are some ways to identify when founders are becoming problematic.

At the start, many board members are picked by founders because they can add money or credibility to the new venture. They are not necessarily chosen to provide serious oversight and accountability. Founders are often strong-minded and persuasive personalities who attract people to a cause. Many times, board members are the first converts to that cause. Founders are frequently able to generate loyalty in their followership that's represented first on the board. So, asking why a founder's board is comprised the way it is can provide good insight into its independence or lack thereof.

Additionally, significant goodwill builds up around founders over the course of a career. This is not easily overcome by early evidence of misconduct. Even when clear evidence of misconduct is present, many followers will continue to defend the founder out of historical loyalty and trust. It's hard to condemn those we like or to whom we feel grateful. It further muddies the water when a founder disputes the evidence. This can result in more confusion and inaction by a board.

Indicators of an unhealthy founder culture

1. Cultural beliefs that the founder is somehow unique, irreplaceable, or in some religious settings, has a special calling from God that insulates a founder from the normal feedback and consequences of misconduct.

2. Cultures that equate agreement with the founder with loyalty to the organization. This produces an environment of compliance that insulate a founder from normal feedback and consequences of misconduct.

3. A system that allows the founder to maintain exclusive relationships with the nonprofit's primary donors, thereby creating dependence on the founder for primary fundraising.

4. Cultures that perpetuate a belief that the organization cannot survive without the founder, and the belief that only the founder knows what is best for the nonprofit.

5. When nonprofit success is overly or exclusively attributed to a founder's activities. Few want to be responsible for taking down a star player. Fewer still want to be whistleblowers, knowing that it's often a long, hard road possibly ending with mixed results.

6. When asset ownership lines blur between what belongs personally to the founder and what belongs to the organization. This blurring can lead to misuse or misdirection of company resources for personal use or gain.

7. A culture that allows the founder to exercise nepotism that goes unchecked by objective hiring practices and supervisory distance between family members.

The impact of complicity

Having worked with many nonprofit leaders, I can attest that nonprofits often reflect the personal characteristics of their leaders, mostly for the better, but sometimes for the worse. Most of the leaders promoted company excellence, commitment to the cause, and modeled self-sacrifice. A few modeled entitlement and arrogance.

When leader misconduct comes to light, people often wonder why it was not prevented or why it took so long to come to light. One reason is the complicity of those around them. Complicity works like this: *People choose to ignore misconduct when they either receive a reward or avoid a punishment for not being oppositional to a wrongdoing of which they are aware.*

Reward and punishment are powerful motivations not to challenge misconduct. People fear disfavor, a loss of status, a loss of income, or some other personal cost that will be exacted for real or perceived disloyalty. People also want the rewards that can be gained through complicity: a promotion, being on a winning team, being close to power, access to a stage or platform, or any other kind of advantage that a bad leader can dole out to people who look the other way. Sadly, the twin motivations for complicity continue to be a main reason today why staff and boards fail to oppose leader misconduct when they know or should know about it.

Responses to problem leadership

Knowing that problem leadership poses a genuine threat to sustainable success, let's get to the solutions. When the problematic behavior is not criminal, unethical, or immoral, *the best remedy is to provide clear and actionable feedback that specifically addresses the problem areas.* Many leaders can grow past leadership mistakes when proven human resource practices are applied, or they receive help from an internal mentor or outside executive coach. Developmental processes like these often lead to better performance, healthier cultures, and longer-lasting leadership careers. It's also the first, best choice for reasons of fairness.

Hire HR professionals and lawyers when needed

If leadership coaching cannot solve the problems, it may be time to seek advice from good human resource (HR) professionals and attorneys specializing in employment matters. I'm surprised how often these options are neglected until the situation gets really messy. Many times, HR experts and lawyers can find ways forward using the terms found in an existing employment agreement, or negotiate a fresh solution acceptable to both parties. It's money well spent, and can prevent a treatable problem from becoming toxic.

Another way to regain management control is to introduce a system of checks and balances around the primary leadership functions inside the nonprofit. These serve to limit the level of authority held by a single leader. Some examples might be to introduce board committee approval for certain decisions, or require multi-layered staff approval for major directional decisions. They might include getting input or sign-off from constituents or outside stakeholders. Placing spending limits is another way to mitigate rogue behavior.

Many nonprofits also find it helpful to use performance appraisal software. There are many good online tools on the market. A list can be found at Capterra.com. Search the site for performance appraisal software.[9] These tools are designed to elicit feedback from people working above and below the leader in order to obtain a report on the leader's strength and weakness. It's important for respondents to believe that they'll be protected from backlash for giving honest feedback to the reviewer. Performance appraisal tools also help managers design higher-performing teams using the collected data.

Explore the value of assessment tools, search firms, and well-drafted employment agreements

Some organizations also find pre-hire assessment tools helpful. There are many online tools, including Gallup's Clifton Strengthsfinder[10] and the Enneagram Institute[11] test. These tests explore the personal strengths of potential leadership hires and can also be used with existing staff. The goal is to ensure that the needs of the organization are matched with the skills and temperament of its future leaders.

Search firms are also widely used to create an appealing and accurate job profile, fill the candidate pipeline, conduct a thorough screening process, and convey the terms of an offer. While there is expense attached to each of these options, it's usually costlier to unwind a poor hiring decision.

I recently served as the co-chair of the search committee for a university president. We employed an excellent search firm. It was fulfilling to have a voice in the future leadership of the institution and be introduced to so many accomplished candidates. The search firm helped immensely by adding a level of discernment that comes only with wide experience matching leaders to specific job requirements.

A careful process that includes good communication, documentation, recorded agreements, and organizational disciplines around accountability serve to prevent hiring mistakes and wrongful termination claims. Doggedly maintaining these practices will pay off, especially in the event of an involuntary parting with a senior leader.

Beyond documenting individual performance, it's important to put the values, practices, policies, and ethics of the nonprofit *in writing*. This step is often missed in smaller nonprofits that are pressed for time and resources. But letting everyone know what actions fall short of community expectations is fundamental to fairness. And it helps leaders perform at their best while maintaining the right level of accountability. What's in writing really matters.

If possible, when a leader departs at the will of the board or retires as planned, it's best to allow him or her to finish well and honorably unless a celebratory sendoff would cast a shadow on the nonprofit's integrity and reputation. Potential successors watch to see how the outgoing leader is treated. Take the high road when it's available.

What to do in cases of illegal behavior

When a leadership failure is related to criminal, unethical, or immoral misconduct, separation will be required for the protection of the nonprofit, its staff and followers. The job of removing a leader belongs to the nonprofit board, which has the legal and ethical responsibility for the proper management and outward expression of a nonprofit. This is a primary reason why it's crucial for board members to understand and take on the fiduciary duty that the role carries. Board members have to be people who are able to make the hard calls. A good resource for board members on the topic of fiduciary duty is *The Nonprofit Board Answer Book* produced by BoardSource.[12]

When a board fails to solve the problem of a leader's wrongdoing, the offended parties may resort to reporting the leader's behavior to investigative reporters or filing a lawsuit. Both of these actions usually result in significant harm to the nonprofit's reputation. This is a compelling reason why boards need to act carefully, correctly, and decisively when faced with complaints of serious misconduct.

In cases of sexual harassment, many organizations set up an internal hotline for victims that connects them to a trustworthy corporate officer or the nonprofit's legal team. Others designate an external oversight group to help victims. The key is to provide the victim with a person and a process they can trust to listen and act to protect them.

Summary of Core Points

- The five common types of flawed nonprofit leadership are: incompetence, narcissistic behavior, abusive behavior, lack of integrity, and irresponsible promotion. Any one—or a combination—of these traits threatens the sustainable success of the organization.

- Founder leaders can go wrong when they fall into the trap of linking their personal interests with the interests of the nonprofit in inappropriate or illegal ways.

- Complicity is defined as the state of being an accomplice to, in partnership with, or involved in misconduct.

- It's the board's responsibility to set expectations and provide accountability for nonprofit leaders.

- Responses to leadership failure include creating good processes around leadership functions and following the competent advice of legal and human resource professionals.

- Performance appraisal software tools can be useful in collecting objective data to help provide accurate feedback and confront unacceptable leadership behavior.

- Consider using pre-hire assessment tools or search firms when filling higher leadership positions.

- Normalize and document performance appraisals for leaders and managers throughout the organization.

- Put all organizational values, practices, policies, and ethical standards in writing and make them widely known.

- If the leader is not receptive to feedback or the failure is related to criminal, unethical, or immoral misconduct, discipline and separation is required for the nonprofit's protection.

- Set up an internal hotline for sexual harassment complaints that guarantees the complaining party privacy and protection.

Coming Up Next

Nonprofit leadership is indeed challenging. That's why leaders who are good at it are in high demand. They have many options about where and what they lead. Therefore, boards need to know how to attract and retain them, and leaders need to know how to find the right fit. When these baton passes are dropped or mishandled, it can jeopardize both the success of the nonprofit and the leader. The next chapter provides tools for boards and leaders to sort out whether a nonprofit job is a great fit for both sides.

CHAPTER 3

STEP 3: FIND AND KEEP GREAT LEADERS

"It's expensive to hire the wrong people. If they leave it's expensive. If they stay it's expensive."

— Nathan Mellor, Sleeping Giants: Authentic Stories and Insights for Building a Life That Matters

"If you can 'hire tough,' you can 'manage easy.'"

— Sue Tetzlaff, The Employee Experience: A Capstone Guide to Peak Performance

What nonprofits need from staff leaders

Because good leadership is in demand, good leaders often find themselves with multiple job opportunities. This includes being invited into nonprofit leadership. But a bad fit between a top leader and a nonprofit is a real threat to the organization as well as to the leader. *Harvard Business Review* reports that, over and over again, organizations are unable to appoint the right leaders. According to academic estimates, the baseline for effective corporate leadership is merely 30%, while in politics, approval ratings oscillate between 25% and 40%.[13]

In America, 75% of employees report that their direct line manager is the worst part of their job, and 65% would happily take a pay cut if they could replace their boss with someone better. A recent McKinsey report suggests that fewer than 30% of organizations are able to find the right C-suite leaders, and that newly appointed executives take too long to adapt. As a result, too many leaders are correctly hired on talent, but subsequently fired due to poor culture fit.[14] The result of a bad fit between a leader and an organization is a lot of pain on both sides. This chapter provides tips for boards and leaders to correctly assess these opportunities, avoid pain, and choose each other well.

A good place for both sides to start is with questions about what the nonprofit needs from the top leader. We've already seen that the first thing every organization needs from its leaders is integrity and emotional health. General Norman Schwarzkopf, commander of the coalition forces in the Gulf War of 1991, put it like this, "Leadership is a potent combination of strategy and character. But if you must be without one, be without the strategy."[15]

Emotional health leads to organizational health

Peter Scazzero's book, *The Emotionally Healthy Leader*[16], is aimed at religious nonprofits but has benefit for secular leaders, too. The *Harvard Business Review* also has many articles and books on the need for emotional health in leaders, and how to develop it as well. In one *HBR* article, Annie McKee writes about the emotional impulses that poison healthy teams. She writes, "I once worked with an executive who was, in fact, blowing up his teams—and his family. He was at risk of losing the prize at work—the CEO job he'd been promised because he got results. The leaders of this company had, thankfully, figured it out. That this guy got results at the expense of every person and team he touched. Naturally, these results weren't sustainable. When I asked him why he did this, he told me straight out: 'I don't care about those people.' Underneath this total lack of empathy was a profound belief that his goals, and his way of accomplishing them, were more important." Here is a great lesson for nonprofits: Results are sustainable only when the overall culture is healthy.[17]

Understanding what makes a leader tick

Nonprofits need leaders to present an accurate self-evaluation of their skills and temperament. Many leaders have taken skills assessments from organizations like the DISC; Lominger Assessment Instruments, Myers-Briggs Type Indicator (MBTI) test or used the Birkman Method. It's wise to ask for the results of these tests or to make them part of the hiring process. These tools inform the hiring nonprofit about a candidate's strengths, temperament, and abilities in an objective way. They won't tell you everything you need to know, but they are helpful with pieces of it.

The first time I took the Clifton StrengthsFinder test, I was surprised by how well it matched with my view of myself and my leadership preferences. I love to take responsibility, think strategically, communicate positively, and get results. In nearly every job I've had, I have been a primary driver. This has been heaven when things have gone well, and a little bit of hell when they haven't!

The truth is, these tools reveal much about how a leader contributes to a team and what kinds of roles bring them joy and energy. Any new leadership opportunity should represent a match between the leader's core strength and the skillsets sought by the nonprofit. Sometimes leaders and nonprofits will agree that a steeper learning curve for a new leader on the job is acceptable. But sometimes circumstances dictate that the right leader is one who can hit the ground running.

Beyond integrity, emotional health, and a core strength match, the nonprofit will need to know whether the nonprofit mission compels the leader's heart and passion. Tepid or ambiguous leadership presents a threat to mission fulfillment because leaders must own the mission as part of the job. Does the leader want to help *this* nonprofit's specific constituency? Does its particular mission excite and capture their best thinking?

Look for a leader with specific passion, not just a passionate leader

A great, related question is whether the candidate is excited about a new leadership role, or whether he or she is excited about *this* leadership role. It's not enough for the job to be challenging, or the compensation appealing. Successful nonprofit leaders "sleep on the cot" for their causes, and those cots get hard and uncomfortable at times.

Power and influence are related but different things

Finally, nonprofit leadership requires leading by influence as well as authority. Can the candidate lead well using only influence? Volunteers and donors respond to persuasion and inspiration rather than command. New generations of employees want a voice in decision-making and proof that they're making an impact. Company loyalty must be earned now more than ever, especially in such a competitive global marketplace and skepticism about leaders in general.

GlobalCourseware says, "Influence is subtle, yet incredibly powerful. You can order someone to do a task, but you cannot order them to do their best. It simply does not work and usually has the opposite effect. You can influence people to do their best by providing a strong, motivating example in addition to positive reinforcement. Leadership addresses tasks, while influence addresses attitudes and awareness. Influence is the soul of leadership."[18]

Executive ability matters

Besides integrity and passion, it's essential to assess a candidate's level of executive ability and whether it's commensurate with the demands of the role. Often, a leader will be hired on likeability or chemistry with the presumption that the executive skillsets are present. Hiring committees need to be objectively exacting when it comes to finding proven abilities.

Of course, this includes conducting thorough reference checks and taking a deep investigatory dive into the evidence of industry expertise. Don't dismiss simple warning flags like job hopping or conflicts with a prior employer. While these are not insurmountable, they create due diligence work for the hiring team. This process is a little like buying a house—it's best not to fall in love with the wallpaper until you've checked the plumbing.

What top leaders need from the hiring nonprofit

Discovering that a candidate is the ideal person for the nonprofit does not necessarily mean that the job is the best fit for them. The nonprofit's need for a leader is not the same thing as a call on the leader's life to fill it. For a job to be the right fit for both sides, it's equally important for the candidate to identify and receive what they need from the role. Arguably, the candidate is in the best position to know whether the job is one in which he or she can thrive.

After the nonprofit extends an offer, it becomes the responsibility of the candidate to dig in, learn everything possible, give serious and honest thought to the future, and decide whether to proceed. While all involved may be committed to correcting a hiring mistake, it's usually disruptive and painful for both sides.

My most recent hiring mistake happened when, as board chair, I was looking to hire a new executive director for the Community Threads thrift store. Because the store depended heavily on volunteer support, I hired someone with a lot of volunteer experience. However, I failed to fully assess her personal orientation to used goods. Because thrift stores normally receive a lot of goods too worn out to be sold and more goods than they can ever sell, a critical part of thrift management is having great horse sense about what to keep and sell, and what to recycle or throw away.

Add to this the fact that most people fall into two categories regarding stuff: hoarders and pitchers. The hoarders want to keep everything ever made, and the pitchers want to toss anything that's not nailed down. My experience is that these two types also marry each other, leading to a lifetime of storage arguments.

In this case, the new executive director was in the hoarder camp, and we were soon drowning in holey t-shirts and chipped china. Here's what every couple knows: hoarders do not become pitchers, and pitchers do not become hoarders. Ever. It's like fingerprints. The new executive director was released in record time, and it was costly all around.

Look closely at who your boss will be, and what's expected of the role

It's been said that people don't leave companies, they leave bosses. Nonprofits have volunteer boards whose primary job is to hire and manage the executive director. Understanding the expectations of that board—and especially the chair—before accepting a role prevents later trouble. The job description should contain the basics, but you should also probe during the interview as to whether there are unwritten expectations.

It's key to know whether the board is unified in its expectations for the role. It's also important to know about the success or failure of the last leader who held the job. Beware of interviewers who focus on all the faults of the last leader. Look for indicators on whether the board is passive or domineering. It's a particular slice of hell to work for a board chair whose goal is for you to be him or her. Finally, assess how the last leader was treated on the way out. Candidates can expect the same treatment when it's their turn.

Discover how the organization defines success

How will the nonprofit measure your success in the position? Are there clear metrics paired with achievable and reasonable goals? Verbal explanations are helpful to understand context, but what's in writing is the most persuasive—at least in a legal sense.

Everyone should have a clear understanding of how success will be measured and rewarded, especially if bonus compensation is tied to achieving goals. If it's not, you might consider asking for a bonus performance plan as part of the compensation package. This will force a conversation with the nonprofit on what it sees as primary objectives for success.

Evaluate the salary, title, and advancement pathways

The salary offer should fall within a reasonable range for similar positions. There are good sources of information available on nonprofit salaries. The Christian Leadership Alliance produces a report on religious nonprofit pay scales. Nonprofits are also legally required to file federal tax form 990s each year, which contain detailed salary information and are publicly available.

Compensation and search consultants routinely research salary ranges to make sure they're both competitive and not excessive. Nonprofit work is demanding, and it's fair to expect to be reasonably compensated for the work. Working for an artificially low salary harms the nonprofit in the long run, because replacement candidates may not be willing to be so generous. It also distorts a realistic budget.

Now is a good moment to have a candid discussion about job titles. While a candidate may have a modest demeanor, titles matter even in the nonprofit sector. Titles should match the level of responsibility the position holds inside the nonprofit. A job becomes harder when the title reflects less authority than the job's level of responsibility.

A good litmus test is whether your title conveys a basic understanding of the job's scope to outsiders. If it doesn't, candidates will find themselves explaining the title over and over. The same goes for goofy, made-up titles. Google and Facebook might be able to pull those off, but generally they're just goofy and made up—and a guarantee for more explanations. Save the title "Grand Master of Underlings" for a Sunday board game.

Candidates should also know about advancement pathways. Sometimes in addition to traditional benefits, a nonprofit will help defray the costs of advanced education. While these are not immediate monetary benefits, they significantly enhance any job offer. Other perks can include a guarantee of work-life balance, limiting travel expectations, and good family leave policies.

Pay attention to the details during due diligence

Take note of how you're treated during the interview process, because things will not get better after you take the job. Board members should remember, too, that they are being interviewed the minute they make that first response to an inquiry.

Typical positive signs are: the interviewers are organized, on time, professionally skilled, and showing genuine interest in you.

Conversely, do they put on the hard sell and talk mainly about what the nonprofit needs? Are the interviews one-sided as opposed to an open dialogue? Flag anything in the interview that makes you feel uncomfortable. Check company reviews online from sources like Glassdoor. They can be revealing, and potentially provide reassurance.

What to do if it doesn't work out

Finally, if you need to make a change—or one is forced on you—try hard not to burn villages on your way out. How you conduct yourself under adverse circumstances will follow you to your next post, and speaks to your leadership maturity and character. Nonprofit circles can be small, and leaders talk at networking, educational, and fundraising events. Leaving well can set you up for greater opportunities. It pays to complete projects as well as you can, give ample notice of your departure, and practice gracious professionalism.

Additional advice for women leaders

Having been a female nonprofit leader as well as managing and representing women leaders as a board member and attorney, I want to encourage the women leaders reading this book to continue to seek leadership roles inside nonprofits. According to MissionBox, "The majority of the nonprofit workforce—more than 75 percent in some U.S. sectors—is female. Still, when it comes to the highest rung of the ladder at big-budget organizations, women are much more scarce. In 2015, GuideStar found that of U.S. nonprofits with annual budgets more than $50 million, just 18 percent had a female CEO."[19]

One of the reasons for this lag, according to Cheryl Sandberg, an executive at Facebook and author of the book *Lean In*, is that women demonstrate less confidence than men. Sandberg says that when a successful male leader is asked how he has gotten to where he is in life, he'll say something like, "Because I'm awesome." Older women leaders tend to say, "I've been so lucky." Younger women leaders often say, "I've worked very hard to get here." It would be great to hear the next generation of women leaders answer this question by saying that they believe they are the best.

At Women Lead's recent leadership conference in California, I spoke with a young woman who lamented that a male colleague who started his job at the same time and in the same position as her had been promoted three times while she had not been promoted once. She related that while she had been encouraged to apply for the same promotions, she had declined because she believed she had not yet gained mastery over her current position. Her male colleague felt no such reservations, and leaped ahead.

Go for it

Kathleen Tierney, an executive with Chubb Insurance, put it this way: "There's never going to be a precisely right moment to speak, share an idea, or take a chance. Just take the moment—don't let thoughts like 'I don't feel like I'm ready' get in the way. Look to see if you have the main things or the opportunity will pass you by. Don't let perfect get in the way of really, really good."[20]

Cheryl Sandberg also describes a double standard applied to men and women leaders. Sandberg says that men are usually liked for being aggressive, bold, and commanding. Conversely, women are often disliked for these same qualities and labeled pushy, hard to please, and bossy. Sandberg says that a woman leader faces a dilemma: she must choose to be perceived either as a good leader, or as a good woman. But this choice is false. Women can be good women and good leaders—and, from my experience, the majority of them are.

Tips for dealing with unfair treatment

Thankfully, issues of gender bias, unequal treatment, and sexual harassment are being exposed and dealt with more effectively than in the past. However, there's still a long way to go. While most companies conduct training designed to prevent unfair or illegal behavior in the workplace, it still happens to both women and men. It's best to draw clear boundaries and not allow others to disrespect you. React to wrongdoing with professionalism. Many workplaces have internal procedures for dealing with bias, harassment, and prohibited behavior which, if trustworthy, can help.

Because these events are already upsetting and potentially career-impacting, be judicious about who you share information with. I suggest creating a response plan in advance that begins by identifying a confidential person such as a therapist, doctor, or lawyer who can provide initial and expert counsel without adding fear that your confidence will be betrayed or misused. Choosing someone who is professionally bound by rules of confidentiality can provide a safe place to process your thoughts and experience.

Place your confidence in competence

Another key value for women leaders is to prioritize competence over popularity. Donna Frosco, President of the New York State Women's Bar Association, puts it this way: "Competence is essential—master your subject matter. You should also have the ability to communicate clearly and adjust your communication for the individual or group you're attempting to reach." Leaders care deeply about mission achievement, and if you contribute well to that, people will want to work with you even if they don't want to be your best friend.[21]

Be strategic about which roles you choose to play

It has also been my observation that women leaders are often utility players. In sports, a utility player is one who can play several positions competently. The concept refers to a player's versatility.

Most women, including women with leadership gifts, learn support skills as a part of growing up female. Consequently, women leaders are comfortable both leading and supporting other leaders. This makes women leaders highly valuable team players. However, in order to avoid getting sidetracked, women leaders should keep prioritizing leadership roles for themselves.

Finally, I advise women leaders to take full advantage of the wider and widening range of choices in the workplace and to support the choices made by other women. There is no one "right way" to have a fulfilling leadership career, so carve out the path that works best for you considering your unique circumstances. And have fun! Having a seat at the table, being able to shape direction and policy, and working on new projects with great people as a nonprofit leader is something the women before you enjoyed and worked hard to secure.

Summary of Core Points

- Too many leaders are (correctly) hired on talent, but subsequently fired due to poor culture fit.

- The first thing every organization needs from its leaders is integrity and emotional health. Character is the one component that organizations must insist upon from its leaders.

- Nonprofits need leaders to present an accurate self-evaluation of their skills and temperament.

- Look for a leader with a specific passion, not just a passionate leader.

- Nonprofit leaders are required to lead not only from position and payroll, but through influence.

- A nonprofit's need for a particular leader is not the same as a call on that leader's life to fill it.

- Every leader must know on day one whether the first priority is to rebuild, or build to the next level.

- People don't leave companies, they leave bosses. Leaders need clarity about role expectations and what it takes for them to win.

- Nonprofit work is demanding, so it's fair to expect reasonable compensation and a title that matches the job's level of responsibility.

- Leaving well with gracious professionalism always pays future dividends.

- Women leaders continue to face additional challenges, including workplace harassment and self-doubt. Several solutions include setting firm personal boundaries, not letting perfect get in the way of really good, prioritizing leadership roles over other roles, and carving out an individualized pathway that best reflects your life circumstances.

Coming Up Next

Problem leaders can certainly wreak havoc. Fortunately, they can be either mentored or replaced. But when the *board* of an organization lacks skills, is passive, interfering, corrupt, or otherwise off course, that creates a serious challenge to the nonprofit's sustainability. Boards are the backstops for making sure things run right inside a nonprofit. Keeping them healthy is essential to success and sustainability. Read on to discover how to keep a board healthy and help those experiencing weakness or breakdown.

CHAPTER 4

STEP 4: BUILD A BETTER BOARD

> *"A Board can be harmonized through leadership humility, insightful business understanding, trustful culture, and learning agility."*
>
> — Pearl Zhu

Building better boards (and fixing broken ones)

When nonprofit operations run smoothly, board service can focus on policymaking, strategic planning, risk management, financial oversight, and succession planning. Nothing in this chapter is meant to dissuade potential board members from signing on to help the nonprofit of their choice, although it makes sense for any potential board member to fully understand the level of responsibility being undertaken. This chapter is intended to help board and staff leaders understand good board play, and how to avoid pitfalls related to board service that other nonprofits have experienced.

A board's capacities and competencies are especially tested when an organization is under stress. Under pressure, the weaknesses and strengths of the board quickly emerge. Boards that are well led, competent, and unified solve problems as they arise and prepare for the unexpected. But when a board is contentious, neglected, or lacking in training or courage, it can splinter under the pressure of crisis management.

The nonprofit leader soon discovers that on top of the problem at hand, there is added complexity at the board level that needs acute attention. Problems at the board level distract the focus of nonprofit staff leaders. To a fraught staff leader, it can feel like being surrounded by fires above and below.

Therefore, it's smart to build the best board possible when things are going well. Because boards serve periodically and at a distance from the day-to-day work of the nonprofit, taking time to build a healthy board is not normally at the top of a leader's list. But, in a crisis, few things matter more than a well-functioning board.

Think of it this way: When a seagoing vessel has good winds and fair weather, the health of the equipment and the proficiency of the crew are required to perform for normal conditions. But when caught in a storm, the age of the ship, how well the radio works, how frequently the engines have been maintained, and the skill of the crew aboard can mean the difference between life and death. The common expression, "All hands on deck!" comes out of this common understanding that in a storm, everybody matters. In the same way, your board's strengths (or lack thereof) will come to the fore when under pressure. Dysfunctional boards create major headaches for their nonprofits. Let's examine some common ways that boards can get off track.

Seven types of broken boards

1. Boards whose members lack the right abilities for the job

A common problem for smaller nonprofits is finding board members with a heart for the cause and the right qualifications. Staff members work best when they can respect a board that's as competent, or more so, than they are. While it's hard for board members to be as *informed* as staff members, they should bring enough executive ability to the table to add consistent governance value to the issues at hand.

Every board has leadership positions. But sometimes the people holding those titles lack the leadership ability needed for the role. A lack of leadership ability in the board chair or executive committee can hinder dynamic staff leadership as well as overall nonprofit growth. When boards fear making a mistake or engage in "analysis paralysis," effective action is delayed and opportunities are missed.

One early board on which I served has a policy that all board decisions be unanimous. Imagine the resulting gridlock and double it! The best board leaders are those who can lead at the board level and refrain from managing at the staff level.

I have heard staff leaders say that the best nonprofits are staff led and board governed. This sounds pithy but, in my view, that maxim has been used as a way to keep leaders off boards for fear of interference. Boards need leaders, staff needs leaders, and they both need clear role definition and the wisdom to stay in their lanes. Depriving boards of good, dynamic leadership leaves the nonprofit vulnerable in times of scandal and crisis, particularly those caused by staff leadership.

2. Boards with the wrong number of members

Boards today need to be both stable and nimble. Board size can vary depending on where a nonprofit is in its life cycle. In the startup phase, a larger board that engages in some managerial functions can be necessary for the nonprofit to get started. When the number of staff grows, smaller policy boards often work well.

The function and size of the board should keep pace with whatever it takes for a nonprofit to stay both agile and stable. It's good practice to conduct a regular review of what is needed from the board and whether the board's current size fits those needs.

3. Passive boards

Passive boards result when expectations for board membership are poorly defined. Good training helps new members know that they're expected to participate in meetings, fulfill their fiduciary responsibilities, and, often, contribute financially. Sometimes boards are passive because they're too trusting, too nice, or too timid. Nonprofits, like hospitals, are filled with good people who want to do good things for other people. Just don't let all that goodness get in the way of members asking the hard questions that boards need to ask.

A lack of rigorous and fair board play, whether generated by ignorance, fear, or kindness, is good soil for mismanagement to grow. A failure to perform board fiduciary duties properly can also subject members to personal or organizational penalties. Prospective members ought to be informed and encouraged to ask questions about how to perform those duties well.

4. Micromanaging boards

Unless the board is actively needed to manage a crisis or is in a startup mode, board members are not responsible for the nonprofit's day-to-day activities. A common rule of thumb is that the board manages the chief executive officer only, and not the reporting staff. Interfering, overreaching, and micromanaging boards can discourage staff leadership teams and defeat the point of using nonprofit funds to pay staff members.

A subset of this kind of board has been called the "seagull" board. These boards have members who swoop in periodically from on high and, with little preparation or information, poop all over the carefully made plans of the staff. Then they swoop out again, leaving the staff to clean up the mess.

5. Nepotistic boards

When too many board members are related to each other, conflicts of interest abound. It is unavoidable that related board members, even the most well intentioned of them, will at some point find themselves at cross-purposes with the best interests of the nonprofit. Some nonprofits are so nepotistic they can be described as family dynasties!

Nepotism also arises when a leadership family desires to retain control over the nonprofit. Just reading this sentence should send a chill up the spine of anyone concerned with independent and unbiased governance. Good governance promotes the mission of the nonprofit over any other interest.

6. Buddy boards

The buddy board is populated with handpicked pals of the executive director or founder. Those close friendships become the main rival to objective governance. The buddy board breeds barriers to true, objective oversight, especially if members believe that being a buddy is more important than what's best for the nonprofit.

Of course, board members can be friends and colleagues. But prioritizing objective oversight is critical for a nonprofit to be healthy. Buddy boards are particularly susceptible to falling into the complicity pitfall as well.

7. Donor-controlled and politically influenced boards

Generous donors are critical to the nonprofit sector. It's natural for them to be invited into board service. This is one of the best ways to include them in the nonprofit's mission. The pitfall is when donor board members get the idea that their donations purchase the right to control the nonprofit's activities. That belief damages the board's objectivity and independence.

Another pitfall is when a board member tries to use board membership as a means of directing nonprofit business to a favored or connected vendor or a job to a favored or connected candidate. Political favoritism has been the source of embarrassment for many nonprofits. At the end of the day, conflicting interests should be guarded against in favor of the pure exercise of fiduciary duty, no matter how harmless conflicts of interests appear at first glance. A good conflict of interest policy is easy to create and implement.

How to build a better board

A good place to start building a better board is to revisit the policies around member selection and board governance. For example, a governance committee could be tasked with a thorough and unbiased board evaluation process, including looking at term limits. A committee report on board health will help dispel any denial of dysfunction. The committee report can be used to mitigate the board's weaknesses and celebrate its strengths. Consider including staff and donors in the evaluation so that the board also finds out on how it's perceived by those it serves. The results can be surprising.

I once served on the board of a nonprofit that was experiencing high staff turnover. The board decided to hire consultants to figure out why. They reported that the staff believed that the board was submissive to the executive director. Consequently, when staff members disagreed with the executive director, they felt they had few options except to leave. Sadly, the staff in this case was correct, and I left the board shortly thereafter because my board colleagues were unwilling to follow the consultant's advice and do what was needed to restore good governance.

The self-led board

Ultimately, it's best for board leadership to lead the conversation about what's keeping the board from full health. It's hard for staff to confront board dysfunction because the board signs their paychecks. Board leaders with courage and conviction must seek the highest-functioning board possible for the good of the organization. That said, it's often staff leadership who feel the pain and know why the board is failing, but have to live with the waste of time and effort it causes.

A lot of things work against board members confronting dysfunction within the board. Sometimes it's a case of denial, or board members may not want to lose friends or be perceived as "the bad guy." There may be fear of reprisals from other board members. When board members are able to put the good of the organization above their personal interests and create positive change, it's a wonderful thing.

Case Study #2: How one healthy board stays that way

Here's how one board that oversees a healthcare network keeps itself healthy. First, it has clear criteria for board member selection and service expectations as essential board-building tools. Existing board members define the skillsets needed for future board composition. That discussion includes a conversation about how well the current board does or does not reflect the desired makeup of the board. The criteria are tailored specifically to the needs of a healthcare nonprofit.

They also have written job descriptions for board members and give special consideration to the duties of the board chair and the officers. Courage and proven leadership are requirements for all board officers. Expectations for the relationship between the lead staff employee and the board are set down in writing. These items are all shared with new members at the beginning of their board service.

In addition to regular board discussions like these, ongoing board training is helpful to energize board members while setting expectations about the privileges and responsibilities of board service. Along with basic board etiquette about meeting attendance and keeping up with organizational communications, board training helps new members understand the work and scope of committees and the difference between managing the organization and acting within board oversight. Housekeeping functions, such as signing the yearly conflict of interest disclosure form, can also be part of yearly training. Finally, governance discussions should include explaining the expectations for board member giving and volunteer service.

It's generally helpful for board members to have had previous board experience, but many boards also take members who require mentoring. However, it's important to know if those with past experience have been well trained by their previous board membership, or if they're coming in with views about board service that are incompatible with your board culture. The Board Source organization provides good screening techniques for new members that will prevent unwelcome surprises in new board members' attitudes or actions.

Board lifecycle

Board function normally evolves with the growth of the nonprofit. Transitioning from a managing startup board to an oversight board can be bumpy for a lot of reasons. Startup board members with a high level of management expertise can find it hard to yield management responsibility to less experienced staff managers. But it also represents early success. It helps to carefully manage board members' feelings of loss and celebrate that success. On rarer occasions, I have seen board members transition from a board role to a paid staff role. This is certainly one way to bridge old and new.

One final way to address board dysfunction is to change the board's governance model. This approach requires a thorough study and broad stakeholder input to guarantee a smooth transition. The Board Effect organization is a good source for information on different kinds of board governance models.

Boards are people, too—treat them with kindness

It pays to keep in mind that charitable board members are mostly volunteers. It's wise to conduct a simple, anonymous survey each year to measure your board members' satisfaction levels. This offers them a chance to confidentially express their opinions about their board service. Let's face it, finding great people who will volunteer their time, donate money, travel to meetings, and take responsibility isn't always easy.

If they do a good job, heartfelt appreciation cannot go wrong. One of the greatest recognitions I received after a time of strenuous board service was the donation from another board member of a week's free stay in his three-bedroom, ocean-front condo at The Montage on Maui for our family. There was no cost to the nonprofit and the gift allowed us to experience a high end vacation on a wonderful property. We felt appreciated beyond measure!

Some typical ways to thank board members for their service include:

- public recognition or an award,

- inviting colleagues to voice words of appreciation at a private farewell event,

- gifts that are meaningful but not excessive,

- mementos or organizational "swag,"

- naming a walkway or building after them, or

- a well-placed commemorative plaque or tile.

How to recruit great board members

Busy people are rarely looking for additional work, volunteer or otherwise. I heard a friend who retired from Nike say, "Work flows to the competent." This is a big reason why poaching executive talent happens often in nonprofit circles for both staff and board positions. In some ways, this is helpful because executives and board members normally increase in skill with each new experience. But it also puts more pressure on the nonprofit leader to make a more sophisticated, value-added proposition to potential board members.

A winning strategy for recruiting a great board member starts with a personal invitation that includes a detailed reason why that person's *unique talents and abilities* are essential to your nonprofit board. This approach reflects a person's need to feel that they are *specifically* wanted and not just that they have a pulse. What is the nonprofit doing that's catnip to this potential board member? How can being a member of your board help fulfill his or her charitable goals? People want to feel genuinely understood and valued for who they are by the organization that's asking for their limited and valuable time.

I was once asked to join a board because more women were needed on the board. Since 50% of the population fit this category, this did not make me feel particularly special. Years later, a good of friend of mine asked me to join another board using the same rationale—but this time as a joke. The same principle goes for invitations to persons of color. While greater diversity should always be a board goal, the invitation to join a board should not be solely based on diversity.

Some boards hold yearly receptions, attached to a board meeting, to cultivate and screen prospective board members. Most boards hold periodic fundraising events that describe charitable achievements and strategic plans. Inviting prospective members to join the CEO's or board chair's table can be fun and fruitful. Sometimes a nonprofit will organize a tour of a facility or an outing as a way to cultivate and screen potential board members. When all else fails, make a date at a candidate's favorite place for lunch.

Create easy on and off ramps for board service

Of course, we all want board service to resemble a long and happy marriage. But sometimes it doesn't work out. It makes sense to build face-saving on and off ramps for board members into your board's routines. There should always be the opportunity for board members to leave gracefully and with dignity.

Board terms are often debated. My personal belief is that a board needs stability, continuity, and enough mandatory turnover that it doesn't stagnate. One way this can be achieved is by staggering three-year, renewable terms for each board member. Board members who serve three consecutive, three-year terms (nine years total) are then required to take at least a one-year break.

Don't forget that future board members and senior staff members will take note of how those who leave are treated. When possible, without sacrificing the trust others have in the organization, take the high road even if a board member or a senior staff person leaves in a disappointing way. Frustrations may run high in the moment, but seeking peace will pay dividends later. Try also to never publicly argue with any departing leader or critic with more ink or bandwidth than you.

Summary of Core Points

- A board's capacities, competencies, and weaknesses are tested when an organization is under stress, so prepare ahead of time.

- The six common board dysfunctions are: boards that lack necessary executive skills; boards with too few or too many members; passive boards; aggressive boards; nepotistic boards; and boards with an agenda that competes with the nonprofit's mission.

- To rebuild an ailing board, revitalize the mechanisms around board selection and governance.

- Board revitalization is best led by the board itself, although staff leadership can play a vital role.

- Healthy boards have clear criteria for member selection and service expectations, together with job descriptions for the board chair and officers.

- Healthy boards conduct board training early and often.

- Healthy boards take care of important housekeeping matters such as conflict of interest disclosure forms, clarity around the financial support required of members, and committee assignments.

- Healthy boards routinely assess and adjust their performance expectations against the life cycle of the organization.

- Healthy boards consider changes to the governance model to address dysfunction or when the old one becomes counterproductive.

- Healthy boards assess member satisfaction levels and remember that members are volunteers.

- Successful recruiting of board members requires making a value-added proposition to prospective board members that takes into account their particular fit with an organization.

Coming Up Next

John Lennon famously wrote, "Give peace a chance." But as he knew well, it's not always easy to find. The Beatles were uniquely gifted. When they successfully collaborated, we all enjoyed the music. But when the conflict got out of control, the band broke up. Read on to learn how organizational conflict is normal and can be used for good if it's well managed. In the next chapter, you'll learn how to keep conflict from taking a destructive turn.

CHAPTER 5

STEP 5: MANAGE DESTRUCTIVE CONFLICT

"The Law of Win/Win says, 'Let's not do it your way or my way; let's do it the best way.'"

— Greg Anderson

Conflict is bad only when it's unmanaged

Many experts agree that conflict naturally takes place when creative people with different opinions, skills, and approaches work together. In fact, some argue that cultures marked by a lack of conflict are in worse shape than those that do have it, because a lack of conflict is evidence of stagnation and low organizational innovation. The bottom line is that conflict inside a nonprofit is unavoidable, and must be well managed or it can tear a good organization apart. Leaders are not expected to prevent all conflict, but they are expected to effectively engage and direct it toward productive ends.

76

It's leadership malpractice to ignore destructive conflict

It follows, then, that leaders who are *conflict-avoidant, meaning unable or unwilling to constructively manage conflict,* are missing a basic leadership competency. Avoidance represents a failure of management resolve. When the leader of a nonprofit fails to confront unhealthy conflict and institute effective mechanisms to channel it successfully, it can seriously threaten a nonprofit's mission. Rochelle Gunn, writing for Mediate.com, says, "dealing with conflict destructively can result in poor decisions, low employee morale, and a tense working environment. Lack of cooperation between teammates and poor information flow interrupts productivity. Successful organizations deal with conflict in a manner that improves rather than destroys staff relationships."[22]

Case Study #3: A nonprofit narrowly avoids imploding over conflict

Consider the case of a multimillion-dollar nonprofit that suffered greatly because of an internal conflict between two senior leaders. They were charged with implementing a two-part mission. Part of the mission was to support sustainable income for people living in impoverished areas, and the other part was to provide job training to area residents. The board believed, as did the executive director, that the two objectives were compatible, possibly successive, but certainly not competitive.

However, each side of the mission was led by very different and equally passionate leaders. They began early on to compete for resources. After years of rivalry, the two became bitter enemies who believed the worst about each other. Because the executive director to whom they reported was conflict-avoidant, the entire staff eventually became embroiled in the dispute and divided into opposing camps. The dual mission of the organization was in jeopardy.

Because the conflict went unmanaged for so long, its presence and effect normalized and brought with it a sense of hopelessness among the staff. Several important staff members left because of the internal bad blood. At last, news of the destructive conflict reached the board, which—after trying unsuccessfully to repair the rift—had little choice but to replace the executive director as well as both senior leaders. A new, dynamic leader began her tenure by defining the nonprofit's missional priorities, bridging the divide between the opposing camps, and working to reestablish trust through a staff-wide conflict resolution process.

This story illustrates all the markers of unhealthy organizational conflict. What began—as most organizational conflicts do—as a personal disagreement between two people, spread into groups of people pitted against each other. The executive director's failure to manage the conflict when it was limited to a dispute between two direct reports shows how resolve and timing are critical elements to successful conflict resolution. Early intervention when a conflict is small and contained prevents a much larger and time-consuming problem later.

The two disputing leaders, unable to resolve the conflict themselves or get help from their boss, failed to recognize that the conflict threatened both their goals and their jobs. Additionally, staff turnover resulted when the toxicity in the upper management spread to the rank and file. Finally, the entire organization suffered from conflict fatigue, a sense of hopelessness, wasted energy and resources, distrust, and collaborative breakdown.

How this conflict could have been managed well

Let's rewrite the story using proven conflict resolution management techniques. In this version, the executive director begins by spotting the serious conflict between two top leaders. He or she then addresses the conflict privately with the two of them together. By asking what steps the disputants have taken on their own to resolve their differences, he or she can understand how entrenched—or not—the conflict has become. They can be reminded of the company values around good conflict-resolution practices, and the importance of putting organizational needs ahead of personal preferences. This is the point where the confusion over resource allocation priority could have been identified and resolved.

If they are still unable to resolve the conflict in a positive way after a check-in appointment, they are offered assistance in the form of a coach, mediator, or internal human resources professional. The goal at this point remains for them to manage the conflict and create solutions for themselves. If they fail in this, more outside intervention may be required.

Ultimately, the disputants will need to find a way to be at peace with each other on a personal level or risk their place inside the nonprofit. Failure to address the root causes for the conflict opens the door to those issues reappearing. Hopefully the resolution of the current conflict will pave the way for other successful conflict resolutions. Many conflicts stem from differences in leadership or communication styles, so if bridges can be built once, they can be used again and again.

If after intervention by the director or a third-party professional the two leaders remain at odds, other creative solutions can be explored, including reassignment of duties for one or both. *The main point here is that leadership needs to persist until the matter is settled.* Making some efforts to resolve the matter is not enough. The conflict needs to be *resolved* before it creates distraction and division inside the nonprofit. Conflict that is left to fester is a threat to organizational mission. Nonprofits thrive when leaders listen well to opposing views, challenge those involved to find solutions that work for the good of the mission, and provide help when needed.

Common root causes of workplace conflicts

Failure to discover and address the root causes of workplace conflict often leads to their return with a vengeance at the worst time. Here are twelve root causes you can use to gauge how susceptible your organization is to destructive conflict:

Poor management. As is clear in the case study above, when people are poorly managed, conflict thrives. Think about it like a sports match without referees. Everyone will make up their own rules in short order, because the rules are neither clearly posted nor fairly enforced. When expectations and processes for handling conflict are absent, polarizing behavior is the predictable outcome.

Inadequate training. Most people enjoy mastering tasks assigned to them, but few will be able to figure out the best way to do new things without some training. Frustrations run high when people have performance goals, especially those that are tied to rewards, without the means to achieve those goals. To avoid conflict stemming from poor training, provide programs or mentoring either online or in person, particularly for newcomers, that clearly explain how people can succeed. Clarity enhances harmony and decreases employee and volunteer stress.

Lack of information sharing. The old saying that "information is power" is familiar because it's also true. Sometimes people hoard information to gain an advantage over coworkers, but most of the time, conflict that results from a lack of information sharing is related to everyone being busy and not taking the time to communicate clearly and fully. Also, the spread of email, text message, voicemail, and a surplus of other shortened communication methods have added to this feeling of being less than fully informed.

One solution is to provide frequent companywide updates on important issues, guidelines for email and text messaging, and regular reminders about how good communication is essential to maintaining healthy teams and cultures. Smart leaders also provide good information-sharing examples, knowing these will keep them out of conflict-resolution meetings and save time in the long run.

Poor communication. Poor communication includes the failure to share information, but also involves any unproductive speaking and writing that causes conflict and misunderstanding. Some examples of poor communication might be sarcasm, hogging time in a group discussion, using too few words, using inflammatory words, monologuing, or overusing annoying filler words like, "You know," and, "Right?" Perhaps you struggle, as I do, to keep these insidious and stubborn fillers out of your conversation.

One effective way of dealing with conflicting communication styles is to make good communication skills a job requirement when hiring. For those already on your team, workplace communication training is a good investment. It also helps to create multigenerational and multicultural teams as a way of building friendships with and respect between differing team members.

Setting up ground rules for written and spoken communications in meetings, including time limits for presenters or using moderators to keep communication flowing well works, too. Of course, it may also be necessary to speak one-on-one with those employees or volunteers whose speech habits raise ire in others.

Bullying or harassment. Bullying and harassment are extreme and illegal forms of behavior that require discipline and consequences rather than training and accommodation. Clear standards and training about what constitute bullying and harassment are important for creating a safe environment for all workers, and a vital exercise for any nonprofit leader.

Limited resources. Sometimes it can seem like the wait to use a shared printer will cause the apocalypse! Limited resources are a main source of conflict in nonprofits, because limited resources are a fact of life for most of them. But charitable employees and volunteers know that the limited resource problem never really goes away because the nonprofit is meeting great needs.

Leadership should create processes that lower the stress around the use and distribution of limited resources and safeguard fairness for everyone. Fairness is key to dealing with this sort of conflict. Most people will understand that a resource is limited, but are frustrated when they feel they do not get their fair share of the resource. By scheduling usage times and amounts of the resource (whatever that may be) in an impartial way, the resource can not only be managed for maximum benefit but also used to create cultural equality and harmony.

Personality conflicts. Sometimes people just don't get along. Personality conflicts are a potent recipe for workplace disputes. In response, a number of tools have been developed to help people understand and relate better to those who think and act differently than they do on the job. As mentioned before, the Gallup StrengthsFinder test describes thirty-four different personality strengths and how those strengths influence the way people work.

Similarly, DiSC by Resources Unlimited 2 helps people discover their personal communication style.[23]

These tools, among others, provide tests and training materials around understanding and working with personality types. The most harmonious workplaces are those that find a way to help their employees understand their differences and how they can blend together for productive ends. Objective tools like these help people see their colleagues' differences as enriching instead of irritating.

Competing or overlapping goals. When job responsibilities are ill defined or overlap, conflict is a natural result. Managers must create clarity around roles and responsibilities, with clear reporting structures. This also works for collaborative or independent work styles. The important thing is to make sure each person knows what it will take for them to succeed. Clear success pathways tamp down conflict.

Organizational change and transitions. The book *Who Moved My Cheese* by Spencer Johnson[24] documents the stress that people feel amidst organizational change. When people feel insecure about whether their job will end, or whether they'll be able to do a different job well, conflict and competition arise.

But change is inevitable in the life of the nonprofit. In an article titled, "Five Powerful Ways to Help Your Employees Cope with Change," *Inc.*[25] suggests that workplace anxiety about change can be reduced by leaders who take the time to watch and listen, demonstrate genuine concern, fix what they can, stay positive, encourage people to look for opportunities in the midst of change, and train employees as early as possible for changes they see coming.

Cultural or generational differences. Jason Dorsey, a researcher in generational kinetics and top millennial speaker, describes baby boomers as watch-wearing, show-up-for-work-on-time people who carry a paper notebook, an extra pen, and shame millennials for taking lunch breaks. Millennials, he says, prize work-life balance, text more than talk, and do not feel the same level of loyalty to employers as workers in the past. Gen X and Y, says Dorsey, have grown up extraordinarily connected to each other through technology but are not tech dependent, are used to being consulted on major decisions, and expect to be promoted quickly. What a diverse workforce facing today's leaders!

Forbes says that leaders who recognize that one size does not fit all, and that their own leadership style is not the only successful style, will take their organizations farther faster than those who seek conformity and style sameness. Victor Lipman, writing for *Forbes*, encourages leaders to, "Tailor your management for each person's strengths, personality and aspirations."

This could be as simple as offering older workers[26] opportunities to gain more skills using technology, or allowing a millennial to work remotely. By leveraging individual strengths, conflict can be decreased. Lipman also encourages leaders to invite newer professionals to take the lead. This gives older professionals a chance to act as mentors and be impressed by the skills of those newer to the team.

The pros and cons of Alternative Dispute Resolution (ADR)

In those rarer cases when employment disputes, such as claims for breaches of contract or wrongful termination arise, many nonprofits have found mediation and arbitration helpful. Most nonprofits include mediation, arbitration, and non-disparagement clauses in their employment agreements to reduce litigation costs, save time, and minimize adverse publicity. Religious nonprofits sometimes have access to conflict-resolution resources through denominational administrative bodies. Mediators and arbitrators can be found through professional organizations like the American Arbitration Association, or locally through bar associations that provide lists of retired judges and lawyers who serve as local mediators and arbitrators.

The results of Alternative Dispute Resolution (ADR), however, are admittedly somewhat mixed. Some of the benefits of mediation include the parties being free to select their own mediator and have an active role in determining the outcome. Also, the results are often more durable than court decisions, and there's less formality than a court hearing. Many ADR processes result in improved relationships.

ADR has its downsides. Sometimes management perceives ADR as an unsuitable deterrent strategy, not reliable for extremely complex factual issues, or cumbersome when money is the only issue in dispute.[27]

However, nearly two thirds of nonprofits in the United States have yearly budgets of less than one million dollars primarily comprised of donations, so including ADR clauses in company contracts often makes good sense. At any rate, nonprofit leaders can benefit by initiating conversations with their boards and leadership teams about how best to manage conflicts that carry legal impact.

More intervention equals less personal control over the conflict

When dealing with conflicts small and large inside a nonprofit, it's useful for everyone in the dispute to recognize that an individual's ability to control the outcome of a conflict decreases with the level of outside intervention required to resolve it. Let me explain. If an offended person can genuinely overlook an offense, meaning to unilaterally forgive and forget it, they are the only one needed to control the outcome of that dispute. When a supervisor, mediator, or HR professional is needed to resolve the issue, the parties retain a say in the solution but are no longer its sole authors.

When the conflict is turned over to an arbitrator or judge, the parties lose all control over the outcome. Someone else decides what will happen. When people understand this loss of control, they're sometimes motivated to settle their disputes early to retain the maximum amount of influence over the outcome of the conflict.

Summary of Core Points

- Conflict inside a nonprofit is inevitable and normal, and must be well managed and put to productive ends so it doesn't become destructive. Successful organizations deal with conflict in a manner that improves rather than destroys relationships.

- Leaders who are conflict-avoidant, meaning unable or unwilling to constructively manage conflict, are missing a basic leadership competency.

- Some root causes for workplace conflicts are poor management, inadequate training, lack of information sharing, poor communication, harassment or bullying, limited resources, personality conflicts, competing or overlapping goals, organizational change, and cultural or generational differences.

- Ways of dealing with these root causes of conflict include:

  o clarifying expectations and processes for handling conflict,

  o providing job training that helps people know what it takes to succeed,

  o providing companywide updates of critical information and creating guidelines for email and texting that promote information sharing,

- o making good communication skills a prerequisite for hiring, setting up ground rules for written and spoken communication in meetings, and creating multicultural and generational teams,

- o eliminating any ambiguity around what kinds of speech or behavior constitutes prohibited harassment,

- o creating fair and unbiased processes for how limited resources will be distributed and used,

- o using tools to promote understanding and appreciation of different personality traits and work styles,

- o creating job descriptions that clearly define roles and responsibilities,

- o communicating well and showing genuine concern during times of organizational change, and

- o committing to the hard work of cultivating more diverse workforces, understanding that "one size does not fit all," and working toward fostering management that's tailored to each person's strengths.

- Many nonprofits include mediation, arbitration, and non-disparagement clauses in their employment agreements to reduce litigation costs, save time, and minimize adverse publicity.

- Greater levels of intervention result in reduced personal control over a conflict.

Coming Up Next

As we've seen, it takes artful effort to get everyone rowing the boat in the same direction. The next chapter deals with what to do if a nonprofit finds itself rowing way off course due to mission drift, and what to do about it.

The balance between keeping up with the times and staying true to the mission for the long haul is challenging for leaders. In this regard, leaders are akin to the coxswain of a rowing team. A good coxswain keeps the boat in the lane, but does so with an easy hand. Steering too much means zig-zagging over the course and rowing far more than 2,000 meters, which adds to time. The trick is to keep the end in sight and steer to a center point far down course. To do this, the coxswain calls out increased pressure for a few strokes on one side of the boat or the other to correct the course rather than use the rudder, which slows the boat down.[28]

Likewise, nonprofit leaders must be aware of mission drift when it occurs and correct it gently and constantly without overcorrecting and losing time. Read on for some great help about how to stay the course but not get stuck in the past.

CHAPTER 6

STEP 6: STAY MISSION TRUE

"This is not about fuzzy, holding hands around a campfire, kumbaya stuff. That's not what values and culture and mission is about. This is about building an organization for success. This is about winning. This is about doing the tactical things to make sure your organization and your people are aligned around the same thing."

— Justin Moore

Why mission drift is a threat

Mission drift is one of the top threats to nonprofit sustainability for two big reasons. First, an ambiguous mission means that no one has a clear sense of where the nonprofit is headed. Mission drift threatens a nonprofit in the same way that the lack of a rudder threatens a boat. Second, changes to a nonprofit's mission can lead to conflict and confusion if not carefully planned and managed. The board of directors has the authority and duty to decide, declare, and defend the nonprofit's mission.

Here's a lesson I learned the hard way during my experience serving on many nonprofit boards: *Maintaining mission alignment is infinitely easier than bringing an organization back from mission misalignment.* It's the difference between driving safely and easily in your lane versus becoming distracted and drifting into another lane, then hearing the loud blare of a horn and swerving wildly back into the safety of your lane. Or worse, it's like driving into oncoming traffic, which only works out well in the movies.

Nonprofit boards have three options regarding the mission: it can remain constant over the life of the nonprofit, be intentionally changed through an organized process, or drift off course over time. Pain will undoubtedly come to the nonprofit leaders and boards who do not "mind the mission" and lead a conversation about changing it *before* it changes. Whenever a nonprofit organization departs from its original reason to exist, whether intentionally or not, it's a huge event in the life of the organization, because where the nonprofit is headed is in doubt.

Why is it important for a charitable enterprise not to lose sight of its mission? According to the *Harvard Business Review*, a well-defined mission or vision statement is one of six components for a great corporate culture. John Coleman writes, "A great culture starts with a vision or mission statement. These simple turns of a phrase guide a company's values and provide it with purpose. That purpose, in turn, orients every decision the employees make. When they are deeply authentic and prominently displayed, good vision statements can even help orient customers, suppliers, and other stakeholders."[29]

Mission drift will happen without intervention

Mission drift will occur without intentional effort to prevent it. Peter Greer argues in his book *Mission Drift* that drift is both natural and inevitable in every organization. He asserts that organizations must establish a clear mission and then combine it with intentional practices that preserve it.[30] Unfortunately, discovery of mission drift usually results in unwelcome repercussions. Recognition that a mission has drifted off course can be deeply alarming to founding members, donors, and others who were unaware that the nonprofit mission was changing without their knowledge, agreement, or input.

Let me be clear: I am not arguing against organizational growth, natural adaptation, and evolution of methods to meet the needs of a nonprofit's clients. I am also not arguing that once a mission or vision is established, it cannot or should never be changed. What I am asserting is that boards should not allow changes to a nonprofit's mission without intention and a careful process with stakeholders inside and outside the nonprofit. I am arguing against the disruption and damage that can result when a charitable mission undergoes transformation that doesn't move the organization forward in a healthy way.

Signs of mission drift

How can nonprofit leaders recognize that a mission lacks vitality and may be drifting? One obvious sign is when key board members or staff cannot easily state what the mission and vision are to someone else. Another sign is abnormal staff and board member turnover, especially if it's connected to a lack of cohesion and unity over where the nonprofit is heading. There may be a sense that the organization is coasting or stagnating. Or you may be faced with a group inside the organization that's pushing the nonprofit in a different direction than the stated mission.

Other signs might be that the nonprofit is facing financial distress due to declining enrollment or clients. A financial downturn could also indicate that the nonprofit's activity isn't as compelling to donors as it once was. In rarer cases, there may be a whistleblower who highlights to outsiders that the nonprofit is no longer fulfilling its stated mission.

Sometimes mission drift occurs when the clients' needs change, and the nonprofit naturally adapts. Take for example the case of a neighborhood community center that excelled for many years in serving a neighborhood immigrant population. Over time that population grew up, and the area needs a teen center now. Some geographically based nonprofits find that they need to relocate or change their mission. The important thing is for the leaders to take time to evaluate, discuss, and plan for how to keep the mission vital and fresh rather than having it die out slowly and painfully.

Case Study #4: the Salvation Army, mission true for 150 years and counting

A great example of nonprofit mission consistency can be seen in the Salvation Army. Organized in 1865 in England, the Salvation Army is a Protestant Christian church and an international charitable organization. The Army's mission is "the advancement of the Christian religion ... of education, the relief of poverty, and other charitable objects beneficial to society or the community of mankind as a whole."

The organization reports a worldwide membership of over 1.7 million. It's easily recognizable today through its homeless hostels, residential addiction dependency programs, children's homes, homes for elderly persons, mother and baby homes, women's and men's refuge centers, general hospitals, services to the LGBTQ community, schools, maternity hospitals, and thrift shops. While remaining a functioning church, it offers services to anyone in need and is integral to the efforts of poverty relief in 131 countries.[31]

Common reasons why nonprofits experience mission drift

There are, of course, many reasons why charitable organizations drift from their original missions. Some of the common ones I've seen are related to rapid growth. When a nonprofit is growing fast, change happens rapidly, too. Personnel are hired quickly to meet new needs.

Sometimes during the interview process, the primacy of the mission and the nonprofit's commitment to it can be diluted, especially when the need to fill positions is great and the competition for hires is strong.

Author and researcher Jim Collins, in his book *Good to Great: Why Some Companies Make the Leap and Others Don't*, argues that determining who is hired—or, as he puts it, who gets on the bus—is more important than a person's particular skillsets.[32] When an organization grows quickly, and therefore hires quickly, it can be difficult to hold the line on whether those new hires are sufficiently passionate about the mission and deeply committed to seeing it thrive.

People can be attracted to a nonprofit for many reasons besides its mission. Sometimes it can be about career advancement. Other times it can be connected to where they wish to live. Sometimes it can be about living near family. None of these are bad reasons to take a job, but when an organization fails to place mission alignment as the top priority when hiring, it will find the allegiance to its mission becoming more and more diluted.

Once nonaligned staff are in place, they'll naturally bring ideas and additional people onto staff who are also not fully aligned with the mission. Additionally, when missionally misaligned people are promoted to higher levels of influence, fidelity to the mission is further compromised.

Neglect and competing values erode mission clarity

Mission drift also occurs when boards and leaders take its adoption for granted and fail to regularly revisit the mission in both public and internally consistent ways. The mission may grow dim in the minds of the staff, and they might wonder about its overall importance. Regular messaging about the centrality of the mission is key to maintaining its vitality.

Sometimes top leaders, arguably the greatest influencers of culture, bring personal or political values into the organization which compete with the mission statement and influence policy. New leaders often want to put their imprint on the organization or leverage their experience and past success. This is fine unless it involves a mission shift.

A recent example of serious mission drift was reportedly discovered by the new top commander of the U.S. Navy Seals, Rear Admiral Colin Green. According to CNN in August 2019, an internal Navy investigation found that members of a U.S. seal team had allegedly abused cocaine and other illicit substances when they were stationed in Virginia. While all members were subsequently disciplined, Rear Admiral Green put plans to grow SEAL teams on hold until he could ensure that platoon leaders were properly trained.[33]

At the heart of the matter was that some SEAL units were placing loyalty to each other above loyalty to the nation. For some, the value of protecting a fellow SEAL took precedence over protecting the interests of the country. Rear Admiral Green took the step of banning the wearing of unofficial unit insignias. It's easy to understand how allegiance to a fellow SEAL, upon whom your life depends, could grow more important than allegiance to the concept of national interest. Rear Admiral Green ended his memo with a quote from former Secretary of Defense James Mattis: "If you aren't aggressive with establishing ethical standards, someone else will fill the vacuum."

Avoid mission clash

Nonprofits are often required to fulfill prerequisites set by donors or spend donor money in a proscribed way as a condition of receiving funding. What has been more recently explored in Greer's book is how these eligibility requirements can impact a nonprofit's mission. The required compliance with a donor's objectives may interfere with a nonprofit's mission in whole or in part. Virtue Ventures, LLC puts it this way: "Problems occur when an organization's enthusiasm to meet its financial goals begins to overwhelm its social mandate."[34] Simply put, nonprofits need to ensure that any conditions set by donors are compatible with their mission.

Religious nonprofits may find this point particularly helpful in terms of avoiding government interference in the execution of their missions. Governmental regulations often follow governmental funding. This was one of the first principles I learned in my constitutional law class. Public funding can also reflect the political views of the party in power and change with subsequent elections, making compliance more difficult.

One Christian college, Grove City College in Grove City, Pennsylvania, is a case in point. To safeguard its religious mission, Grove City College offers its students private loan opportunities with local banks and works hard to keep its tuition costs low as a way to minimize student dependence on government aid programs. This strategy protects Grove City's mission from governmental interference related to public funding.

Many nonprofit organizations are evaluating not only where money is coming from and what strings may be attached to it, but also asking questions about how the nonprofit's money is being invested in light of mission alignment. There's a new emphasis on congruence between the nonprofit's mission and its investment policies. More and more nonprofit stakeholders are looking for indirect as well as direct mission fidelity. The sole concern with financial return on investment is fading. Nonprofits can receive assistance for this kind of evaluation from organizations like the Intentional Endowments Network, which helps mission-driven organizations incorporate sustainability into their endowment decision-making.[35]

We measure what we value

A failure to measure the indicators of mission alignment can contribute to mission drift. Measuring mission alignment is harder than measuring other success indicators, like attendance and dollars, which is why it's so often neglected. Some nonprofits measure how often their clients engage with them year over year to gauge mission awareness. Others conduct surveys aimed at assessing client and donor satisfaction with and understanding of the mission. Some count how often the mission statement is contained in the nonprofit's public messaging.

Seven ways keep your mission on track while being open to change

1. Begin with a board conversation

What, then, can be done when mission drift has occurred and the nonprofit is experiencing a loss of donor support, abnormal staff turnover, a lack of directional focus, or another unwanted consequence? Begin with a board conversation about the necessity for mission clarity. The board has the responsibility to set a clear and unambiguous direction. Mission clarity is essential to that duty. It's not uncommon for differences of opinion to be discovered inside a board itself if board members have been added to the organization without a proper emphasis on or understanding of the organization's mission.

2. Engage in a robust stakeholder dialogue

This board discussion should be closely followed up within senior staff, who should evaluate the level of unity and cohesion around the current mission. If mission drift is suspected, a process of renewing, clarifying, or changing, the mission will be needed.

It is wise for this process to include a robust dialogue with stakeholders. Mission statements are usually discussed at a high level. However, as more individuals are invited to discuss what each word means and how it will be achieved, differences of opinion may quickly emerge.

Discussions about mission are similar to political discussions about lowering taxes. Everyone quickly agrees that taxes need to be lower. But the specifics about *how* those taxes will be lowered is where the rubber meets the road.

3. Evaluate unity around the mission

It's difficult for a board to impose and enforce a mission statement on a divided rank and file. It will take considerable consensus-building to ensure that the mission is once again well defined and embraced at all levels among board, staff, and supporters. Without unified buy-in, nonprofits cannot achieve real congruence on their mission.

4. Locate historical and legal sources that defined the mission

In legal terms, the mission of a nonprofit is normally found in the organizational documents such as the bylaws or organizational charter. Early publications from when the nonprofit was formed can provide context. Employee or faculty handbooks are additional sources. Mottos, value statements, and identity statements may also reflect the original intent of the nonprofit's charitable purpose and add to the current conversation.

5. Allow for a new but separate mission to arise

By conducting a healthy conversation around mission value and unity, it's wise to consider what will happen to the organization if the mission is either affirmed, modified, or abandoned. While some inside the organization may want a new mission, if the board or donor base does not, perhaps starting a new organization with a new mission is the right step for that group. The nonprofit can then shift emphasis toward how the dissenting group can leave well, in a way that honors both sides. Many good nonprofits start as an offshoot of another one.

6. Generate great mission maintenance

Some organizations, once the mission has been reclarified, have taken the step of hiring a specific executive or leader to be the chief mission officer who will maintain it. The role's purpose is to ensure that the mission is represented in each of the nonprofit's major strategic decisions. Some would argue that this responsibility already belongs to the CEO or president. Others argue that creating a position to specifically champion the mission has the reverse effect of diluting everyone else's missional commitment. The point, however, is that for mission drift to be effectively avoided, the organization must intentionally plan ways to preserve it.

Sometimes a conversation about mission alignment will reveal that the organization's leader or leadership team are not aligned with the original mission. They may have ideas about where the nonprofit should go in the future that represent a different direction from the board or donor base. If the board agrees, the organization's mission can change. But if not, the lack of alignment will likely result in either staff or board member changes. This need not be acrimonious, but it does need to be clearly identified and addressed so the nonprofit is not being led in a way that results in directional cross-purposes.

7. Fix a mission that has drifted

Once mission drift is discovered, and if it's displeasing to those governing and leading the organization, it will take courage and commitment to right the ship. Mission drift normally happens over a long period of time, and likely involves significant investments by people who love the organization but desire to take it in a different direction. Unwinding these relationships, partnerships, and—in some cases—friendships can be difficult. However, once mission drift is uncovered, the choices are clear. Either the organization must return to its original mission and all it entails, or it must realign itself with a changed or new mission in order to stay cohesive and effective.

In summary, it's very easy for smart board members and leaders to become distracted and neglect to guard the organization's mission. It's also easy to be in denial that mission drift has occurred. The way back to mission alignment will take time, and may engender feelings of betrayal on many sides before consensus is reached and the nonprofit can move forward in unity. But mission ambiguity is worse.

Summary of Core Points

- An ambiguous mission means that no one has a clear sense of where the nonprofit is headed.

- A nonprofit board has three options regarding its mission: it can remain a constant over the life of the nonprofit, be intentionally changed through an organized process, or drift off course over time.

- Maintaining mission alignment is infinitely easier than bringing an organization back from mission drift.

- It makes more sense to be intentional about changes to the mission rather than allowing it to change as the result of neglect or drift.

- Signs of mission drift include board and staff members being unable to readily and accurately describe the mission, abnormal staff turnover, lack of directional cohesion, flagging donor support, and the presence of a whistleblower.

- Things that contribute to mission drift include rapid growth and hiring, leadership nonalignment, competing priorities, irregular messaging about mission, donor directives that compete with or contradict the stated mission, and mission obsolescence.

- Mission realignment begins at the board level, but must involve robust dialogue with all stakeholders.

- It's difficult for a board to impose and enforce a mission statement if there has been significant departure from it within the rank and file. It will take consensus-building to ensure that the mission is once again well-defined and embraced at all levels among staff and supporters.

- To effectively avoid mission drift, organizations must intentionally plan ways to preserve it, including assessing stakeholder fidelity, communicating its importance, including mission alignment in all hiring decisions, and measuring how the mission is being effectively advanced.

- Either the organization must return to its original mission and all it entails, or it must realign itself with a changed or new mission in order to stay cohesive and effective.

Coming Up Next

What kinds of workplace norms and habits attract great performers? How can a nonprofit with limited resources and a smaller staff retain the best people? What makes a workplace "sticky?" The next chapter contains great tips of the nonprofit trade for hiring and retaining the best talent out there, and not losing the great talent you already have.

CHAPTER 7

STEP 7: DEVELOP A LOYAL STAFF

"I consider my ability to arouse enthusiasm among my people the greatest asset I possess, and the way to develop the best that is in a person is by appreciation and encouragement. There is nothing else that so kills the ambitions of a person as criticism from superiors. I never criticize anyone. I believe in giving a person incentive to work. So, I am anxious to praise but loath to find fault. If I like anything, I am hearty in my appreciation and lavish in my praise."

— Charles Schwab

Finding great staff members and volunteers is an ongoing challenge for nonprofits. But the loss of key staff members and excessive staff turnover magnifies the challenge. Replacing them wastes precious nonprofit time, energy, and resources. Anything that drains those three interferes with sustainability.

Here's why. Nonprofits are often looking for candidates who are specifically qualified to work with its clientele. Candidates are usually required to have the applicable educational degrees, experiences, and temperaments that correspond to the way a nonprofit delivers help. For example, hospitals hire people with medical training, and schools hire people with educational training.

Also, nonprofits typically have a smaller staff and therefore depend more heavily on the talents of a few. Losing a "pillar person" hurts morale and temporarily reduces the overall effectiveness of the team. Remaining staff must pick up the slack, and that puts them at risk for burnout.

Nonprofit work is also a traditional stepping stone and training ground for younger professionals who plan to eventually move to other markets or start their own businesses. For this reason, nonprofits expect a higher turnover in their ranks. However, when that turnover becomes excessive, the interrupted momentum becomes costly to the organization. These time and money costs pose a significant threat to mission fulfillment. This chapter provides proven tips to attract and retain high-quality employees, minimize excessive turnover, and stand out as the workplace of choice.

Play your best hand: emphasize your powerful mission

A lot of great people choose to work for a nonprofit because they want to make the world a better place. So the most powerful recruitment tool for any nonprofit is to compellingly convey an attractive mission to likeminded job seekers. Many employees will choose to work for a nonprofit that shares their religious convictions, political views, or patriotism. Your cause is your best calling card. Make it work for you in the job market. Millennials already comprise 50% of the American workforce, and are drawn to social causes more than past generations.[36]

Let's take a second look too at a few marketing fundamentals that nonprofits sometimes neglect. Job seekers today commonly use technology as a primary way to connect to the world. This phenomenon can help smaller nonprofits reach out to them more easily and for less cost than previous workforce recruitment methods. Good online ad placement and updated messaging formats signal to newer professionals that your nonprofit is current.

These marketing principles may seem basic, but many nonprofits fail to budget for online recruiting, website updates, or video content creation. But there are a number of ways to create crisp and clean brand presentation inexpensively. Websites like WordPress, Bluehost, Wix and Squarespace offer free website templates, while Fiverr.com offers design services at a range of reasonable prices.

Workplace reviews on Google, Amazon, Glassdoor, Indeed, and LinkedIn matter, too. Even though some review sites have a reputation for posting mainly complaints, they still hold influence. While no one should post or encourage others to post fake reviews, a nonprofit can remind its staff, friends, and donors to create positive reviews if they have a genuinely positive opinion. Poor reviews and ratings hurt more than some leaders realize. Working to keep those reviews current and positive helps with recruiting, and if there are genuine reasons why your nonprofit is receiving negative reviews, it is important to find out why.

Use data to demonstrate your organization's positive impact

Prospective employees will want to know how well a nonprofit is doing at achieving its goals. People want to be part of a winning team. Today's younger workers seek impactful, welcoming workplaces and a paycheck, often in that order. Presenting how the mission is being accomplished with verifiable data will win—and keep—the hearts and minds of your best employees. Not all nonprofits can boast enormous success, but most can show progress and achievement in the face of challenge. Highlight regularly all the ways your nonprofit is making progress.

Nonprofits providing relief in hazardous or challenging environments have an extra hurdle in recruiting staff. Interestingly, nonprofits like Habitat for Humanity and World Vision succeed in attracting and retaining top employees even though some personal risk is part of the job. Habitat consistently ranks high on the list of nonprofits people want to work for. The number one reason for this is Habitat's supportive managers and opportunities to learn transferrable skills. Habitat teams experience community while being productive.

Offer important non-monetary perks

Karsten Straus writes in *Forbes* that the feeling of being valued, having a chance to develop unique skills, and connecting with important networks attracts the best candidates. Providing employees with rewards other than money, such as a chance to develop a second language or learning to thrive in a diverse culture, are proven recruiting and retention tools.[37]

It's also smart to advertise that nonprofits often provide greater job security for employees. As they grow, nonprofits can offer pathways for advancement even if those pathways may take a bit more time. Nonprofits also increase employee satisfaction when they find non-monetary ways to recognize employees for their contributions and create a sense of family.[38]

Public personal recognition is also meaningful. Singling people out for special credit is generally more effective than making a sweeping thank you to a group. Of course, this runs the risk that someone else will feel overlooked, but that's just life. A personal note of thanks goes a long way. No employee has ever complained or left a job because they received too many compliments, awards, or rewards.

Whenever possible, it's smart to include employees in important decision-making processes. Having a meaningful say in the direction of the organization increases employee ownership and encourages them to take responsibility for company success. Nonprofits that create dynamic teams empowered to set direction on specific projects have higher retention rates than those whose employees are expected to follow orders and work in silos. Good strategic planning processes that invite broad employee input are a great way to create deeper investment.

Finally, look for those people who make other people want to stay. They are sometimes the overlooked heroes. One of Community Threads' best thrift store managers always brought homemade cookies to work on staff members' birthdays. She was very important to group morale. In *Business News Daily*, Jennifer Post writes, "A positive attitude is important for many reasons, but one of the main reasons for having a positive attitude in the workplace is because it can rub off on everyone else."[39]

Manage workplace conflict and reward excellence

The converse of this is even truer. Unproductive workplace drama is a culture killer. Conversely, culture thrives when good conflict-resolution methods are practiced, and healthy disagreement is channeled into a productive creative process. Meanness and intolerance not only discourage people, but they may be legally actionable. Good leaders set reasonable standards for behavior and prevent the devaluing of people as well as the brand.

Unfortunately, when working with various nonprofits I have noticed with some regularity a pattern of not paying some of their most loyal and hardworking employees at market rate, or paying squeaky wheels more than the silent faithful. This bothers me. It's unfair and counter-cultural to presume the good nature and high commitment of loyal employees. While it is true that people should speak up for themselves about their wages, compensation parity is important to legal compliance and considerate of equal effort.

Now I'm going to throw a little fat into the fire. Once your nonprofit has a fair and published pay scale, pay your highest performers as much as you can. I am not advocating for unequal pay for equal work. What I am saying is that, in certain instances, it's smart to pay more to people who perform *in exemplary ways and contribute at higher levels* so as to keep those star performers working in your organization. Compensation is usually key to that.

Case Study #5: Google's method for defeating hiring bias and maintaining consistent quality

Multiple studies have shown that employee interviews are negatively affected by "hiring bias."[40] It has been noted that most interviewers make the decision to hire or not the first ten minutes of an interview. Bias creeps in, especially when hiring managers have a picture in mind of a certain person, or personality, they believe best fits the role.

In order to combat this natural bias, Google uses a hiring committee that's independent of the direct management of the new employee. Google wants to ensure consistent quality in hiring by using objective company standards for every hire. The hiring committee focuses on skillsets that the company values rather than on those a single manager believes are required for the role.

The committee also looks at the team's current composition for what is missing. With preset company standards inserted in each and every hire, maintaining overall objective quality improves over time. It has been shown that using independent committees eliminates much of the bias that leads to early employee failure and termination.

Another technique that has proven useful to ensure that those hired will be a good fit for the organization is the multi-layered interview system. Better hiring and longer tenure have resulted when candidates are interviewed by employees working in unrelated departments and at various levels within the organization.

Finally, a number of studies have shown that a diverse workplace increases profits and produces a more stable work environment. Time and time again, when people feel like they are a solitary voice inside a workplace, they will seek employment where they do not feel quite so alone. While a more diverse workplace requires staff to adapt more to differences, it also yields better organizational outcomes and is worth the extra effort.[41]

Qualities to look for in nonprofit employees

Are there specific qualities that work better in a nonprofit setting? I believe so. Here are eleven that are important in any charitable work setting:

1. **High integrity.** Because trust is at the heart of all nonprofit success, integrity is a required quality for anyone hired by a nonprofit.

2. **Commitment to the cause.** While commitment to the cause cannot supersede solid abilities, tepid enthusiasm for the nonprofit's mission is also a deal breaker. It's a mistake to hire someone with antipathy toward the mission. That lack of enthusiasm will surface over time in a million small ways. It's also irritating to the staff who are "all in."

3. **Mission keeper.** The people who carry the cause in their souls, show up at every event, speak up when others do not, defend leadership when unfairly criticized, and find hope in the darkness are mission keepers.

4. **Hard worker.** The hard worker understands that success— as Thomas Edison, inventor of the lightbulb, so aptly said—is ten percent inspiration and ninety percent perspiration.

5. **Chemistry and camaraderie.** Nonprofit teams can be small and work in tight physical spaces. The ability to get along well in any team is a prized trait in new hires.

6. **Resourcefulness.** Because resources are typically in short supply in nonprofits, the ability to creatively adapt to different circumstances is a great quality in nonprofit employees.

7. **Respectful of differences.** Staff members who are able to make positive interpersonal connections with a variety of people and show consistent respect for others help nonprofits reach greater audiences.

8. **Reliable.** Perseverance, punctuality, and an ability to plan ahead adds up to a person who can be counted on. Nonprofits serve many people in need who depend on their services. Staff members cannot flake out.

9. **Able to communicate wisely.** Nonprofit employees often come into contact with confidential or sensitive information. It's important for employees to be able to keep those confidences, speak kindly and clearly, avoid rumors and gossip, and use appropriate discretion in their wording.

10. **Open to learning new things.** The attitude of a learner is a desirable trait in nonprofit employees. Employees who are willing to be taught by newer professionals or to learn from experienced mentors helps grease daily interactions.

11. **Bravery.** Most nonprofits tackle formidable and intractable problems. Hiring people who exhibit courage in the face of setbacks, who can regroup after disappointments, and rally others to not give up are worth their weight in gold.

Handle staff departures with grace and honor

A highly talented and well-educated friend of mine took a job working for a nonprofit as the second-in-command to cross-train before becoming the president of a larger company. He committed to spending two years at the nonprofit, and during that time proved himself highly effective and likeable. Six months before he was scheduled to leave, the president offered him large incentives to stay on. But he declined, having already given his word to lead the other organization. The disappointed president took the rejection personally and made his feelings clear over and over again during my friend's last six months. These antics did not work and diminished the president's leadership credibility with the remaining team members.

As hard as it is, there will be times when people who are important to the mission's achievement leave. And frankly, whether voluntary or involuntary, departures like these can set an organization back for a time. This is especially true if the nonprofit doesn't receive much notice before the departure. But it really pays to take the high road whenever possible. Other employees will be watching. Who knows if the departing employee will become a donor or a valuable connection? At least try to keep a friend.

The best response when someone beloved or important leaves is to acknowledge the loss with his or her colleagues, acknowledge the reasons why the parting is hard, move forward with good communication, celebrate that person if appropriate, and take the time necessary to find the right replacement. A key departure may offer the chance to rethink a role, assess what's needed for the future, and conduct a thorough search. An exit interview conducted by a third party can help the departing person be candid about ways the organization can improve. Some organizations find it helpful to hire an interim leader to create stability before moving on with the next longer-term hire.

Finally, it may be a great thing for your nonprofit to be known as a CEO factory. General Electric had that reputation for many years, having produced at least sixteen executives under GE CEO Jack Welch. More recently, Amazon is being credited by the *Wall Street Journal* as the next for-profit company to produce a high number of CEOs from within its executive ranks. Dana Mattioli wrote for the *Wall Street Journal* that Amazon's executives are spreading the giant's scrappy mentality throughout the economy and leaving the harsher parts of its culture behind.[42]

Summary of Core Points

- Loss of key volunteers and staff is a threat; it wastes valuable and limited time, energy, and resources.

- A compelling mission, winsomely presented in contemporary ways, attracts today's best and brightest board members, leaders, and staff.

- People root for underdogs, but they follow (and want to work for) winners.

- Nonprofits who make their employees feel valued, give them a chance to develop unique skills, experience a culture diversity, and work with supportive managers have the highest rates of employee retention.

- Nonprofits that pay fairly, prevent unproductive workplace drama, and express appreciation not only steer clear of legal troubles but also cultivate employee loyalty.

- It's good practice to reward exemplary employees with commensurate rewards.

- Hiring bias can be prevented with methods such as hiring committees, multi-level interviews, and objective goals around gender and diversity.

- The loss of a key employee is difficult for any nonprofit and should be acknowledged, handled with grace, and recognized as an opportunity.

- Ultimately, the desirability of a nonprofit's staff to other organizations is a compliment that can spread a nonprofit's influence and reputation.

Coming Up Next

Finding future great staff leaders takes a lot of time. Add to that other management issues and time spent in strategic planning, it's no wonder there's little time left for boards and executive directors to pay attention to future trends and innovative competitors. How can nonprofit leaders prevent waking up one day and finding the world has moved on without them? Good news! The next chapter addresses ways that nonprofit leaders can stay sane, current, and set up for a preferred future now.

CHAPTER 8

STEP 8: INNOVATE, IMITATE AND STAY AHEAD OF THE CURVE

> *"Learning and innovation go hand in hand. The arrogance of success is to think that what you did yesterday will be sufficient for tomorrow."*
>
> — William Pollard

Keeping up with important trends

It's difficult for busy leaders to stay current on trends that can impact a nonprofit's mission. New legislation, advancements in technology, and creative "competitors" are just a few of the ways the nonprofit landscape constantly changes. Surprises like these can jeopardize nonprofit sustainability. This is why innovation blindness is listed here as one of the top threats to sustainable success. This chapter is aimed to give you ways to keep current, stay ahead of the game, and adapt to trends in a timely way.

The following are some examples of nonprofits that are paying now, or have paid big prices for failing to keep up with discoverable trends. Consider the many enrollment challenges facing American colleges and universities today. For years the cost of higher education has been on the rise. Boards of trustees have continued to approve budgets with tuition and fee increases to cover the rising cost to educate. Eventually, student tuition and fees exceeded what the average family income could reasonably afford, at the same time the number of available students in the pipeline shrank. The current challenges to higher ed's sustainability including declining enrollment and cost inflation have been indicated for some years, but went largely unaddressed until now.

Learning lessons from the higher education crunch

Because of the cost of higher education, rising student debt, and static post-college income, parents and students have focused more on college alternatives. They have started asking whether a college degree is still essential to career success. Local community colleges and for-profit colleges have arisen as formidable competitors to nonprofit colleges and universities by offering core education courses for lower costs while allowing students to live at home.

A few colleges who can afford it have begun to offer free tuition. New York University, for example, raised enough money to offer a medical school education for free. Students and parents are laser focused on the prospect of getting a good-paying job post-college. Getting a good job post-college is a new primary driver in student choice for education. Alumni employment rates are now measured nationally in the United States, and will remain an ongoing litmus test for how well colleges are serving their students.

While this may seem like a crisis that came out of nowhere, the factors exerting pressure now on the nation's colleges and universities have been on the horizon for a while. Most boards missed them or did not react fast enough and are now seeking ways to cut costs, deliver courses more efficiently, appeal to nontraditional students, and form collaborative partnerships.

The trustees that did see the rising costs coming worked to raise funds for endowments that are helping their institutions weather the storm. Some offer more scholarships and higher discount rates on tuition costs. Some are partnering with high schools and community colleges to provide early college credit. Most colleges and universities now offer some form of online program. The recent worldwide viral health emergency threw even the most conservative colleges and universities into a giant online learning experiment. The lessons coming out of so many students learning online at once will shape how much and how well online learning is done in the future.

Another type of nonprofit dealing with changing times is one which has primarily relied on revenue from conference attendance fees. In the past, many professionals enjoyed traveling to attend conferences for training. Often, they could combine networking opportunities with a training or sales event. But fewer people today want to take the time to attend a multi-day conference because of increased overall demands on their time, the ease of finding the same content online, and more recently, health concerns.

Technology has of course played a huge role in bringing conference content materials conveniently online and removing the need for travel. While there may always be in person conference events, even the strongest vendors are looking for ways to create more value for their attendees by keeping them engaged between the big events.

Case Study #6: Great organizations can still miss clear opportunities

Rotary International is a worldwide nonprofit with over 100 years of distinguished membership and accomplishments. In 2017, the Gates Foundation announced a partnership with Rotary on its critical work toward the worldwide eradication of polio. This expanded agreement will translate into $450 million for polio eradication activities, including immunization and surveillance over three years. This critical funding helps ensure countries around the world remain polio-free and that polio is ended in the remaining three endemic countries: Afghanistan, Nigeria, and Pakistan.[43] Rotary has been a sustained success.

However, Rotary International's history of defending its status as a club only for men serves as a cautionary tale. In 1987, when women were joining the executive ranks in record numbers, Rotary engaged in a lawsuit about whether it could, as a constitutional right, remain an all-male club. The U.S. Supreme Court ruled that in states where the Equal Rights Amendment had been adopted, Rotary Clubs could not exclude women members.[44]

The Supreme Court decision recognized that the Rotary Club was not only a nonprofit, but also an important point of commerce for its members. Club meetings were not only a place to promote and organize civic good works, but also a place for members to network and conduct business over breakfast or lunch.

Today, over thirty percent of Rotarians are women. With the surge of educated women entering the workplace and achieving corporate leadership positions in the 80s, one could argue that it would have been more strategic for Rotary to have welcomed women rather than engaging in costly litigation to keep them out. But even sustainable organizations can miss clear opportunities. And it remains to be seen whether Rotary will continue to attract as many members in the future.

Here is my personal story with Rotary. When I was a fifteen-year-old high school student, I was privileged to be selected as a Rotary exchange student to Australia. I spent a wonderful year of learning and gained an invaluable appreciation for life outside the United States. Later, in the 80s, Illinois passed the Equal Rights Amendment when I was newly admitted to the bar. I felt a deep connection to Rotary, but I could only hope to be a "Rotary-Anne"—the wife of a Rotarian, not an actual Rotarian.

A lawyer friend, knowing of my interest, proposed me for membership after the Supreme Court ruling was published. I became the first female member of the Libertyville Rotary Noon Club and I was warmly welcomed. Through Rotary, I was able to start an Interact Club at the local high school which allowed more teenagers to become exchange students. For me, my Rotary experience came full circle and I admire all the good that Rotary still does today.

The Rotary case study shows the importance of keeping up with societal trends and adapting to them. The threat of being left behind is real for nonprofits. Read on to discover what kinds of actions you can take to stay to keep your organization sustainable in changing times.

Balancing innovation with the "tried and true"

According to Knut Haanaes, the dean of the Global Leadership Institute at the World Economic Forum, the best way to stay strong in the present and be prepared for the future is by finding the right balance between risk-taking, discovery, and innovation while continuing the practices that have historically been the "tried and true." Haanaes says there are two main reasons companies fail at innovation: either they *only do more of the same thing, or they only do what's new.*

Keeping exclusively to what has worked well in the past leads to obsolescence. But at the same time, overcommitment to innovation or exploration leads to failure because of the "trap of the perpetual search." Companies overcommitted to innovation come up with ideas, but don't stick with them long enough to make them a success. Haanaes says studies show that only 2% of companies are able to find the right balance, but when they do, the results are extraordinary, and the payoffs are huge.[45]

Why do leaders fail to focus on innovation? Part of the reason is that innovation happens less as companies age, especially if they're successful. Bill Gates says, "Success is a lousy teacher. It seduces us into thinking we cannot fail."[46] Older companies generally have more successful products to exploit, and therefore become complacent about innovation. Eventually though, they run out of things to exploit and find themselves without something new to offer the world—just when their competitors do.

You might well ask then, somewhat despairingly, if an international group of successful business leaders like Rotary International could not discern and take advantage of the predictable rise of women leaders in the workplace, how can the rest of us ever hope to read the tea leaves well enough to keep our nonprofits from becoming obsolete? The answer is to first believe that your nonprofit *can* become outdated. This is the first mental hurdle to jump.

Nonprofits experiencing more and more success have a hard time imagining a downturn just like for-profit companies do. And that unbelief is the great precursor to a fall from grace. Once you can imagine what it will take for your company to lose its edge, you can begin to move against that event.

Then, take note of the places where you're most vulnerable to change or where your peers are innovating. Are there areas of your organization where yellow caution lights are blinking and demand is weakening? Start there and have some fun dreaming.

Don't rest on your laurels

Will your company's greatest strength be a strength in five years? In ten years? What if this strength is resting on the talents and abilities of one person, or on a small but aging team? Is it possible to diversify and prepare for that person or that group to move on? What about doing a good old-fashioned SWOT analysis at the next retreat? So much of this is about taking the time to be situationally aware, to ask the hard questions, to slaughter the sacred cows, and begin the hard work of renewal planning.

By giving your staff permission to carve out precious and dedicated time to read and listen to resources, chances rise that someone will come across a trend that matters. Try not to limit your research to what is only in your field of service. Consider dedicating board time twice a year to ask where your mission is headed. Challenge the assumptions that have worked for your nonprofit for a long time but could be at risk.

Leaning into the next gen and saving for a rainy day

Another strategy to keep current is to recruit and really listen to what your next generation of employees are saying about your organization and trends. Ask them what they're reading, who they're listening to, and what matters to them on their podcast lists. Ask them plainly whether they have ideas to keep the nonprofit engaged with younger age groups and how well the company is doing speaking about issues that matter to them.

If possible, do all you can to financially prepare for the inevitable rainy day. When surprised by social, geographic, or political changes, a rainy-day fund can help buy you enough time to breathe and create a successful recovery plan. Try also to stay informed about any financial trends in and around your location. Geography has a big impact on sustainability. Are higher taxes on the space you rent imminent? Is your area gentrifying so that rent rates are likely to increase? Is local government regulation that will make your nonprofit less viable on the horizon? Are your donors aging, retiring, and relocating to warmer climates?

Don't be afraid to consider a merger or to imitate

Another proven strategy for preventing stagnation is to embrace the habit of importing talent and products from "the outside." Some of the best examples of this strategy can be found in the pharmaceutical industry. Pharmaceutical giants like Pfizer and AbbVie are known for their success in internal discovery. However, they also have a robust track record of incorporating startup biotech firms and hiring their innovators to swallow the competition and stay competitive.

Small and large nonprofits can also use this strategy. By hiring talented people who are exhibiting fresh thinking and risk-taking where they lead, nonprofits can import innovation. To attract these individuals or newer nonprofits for collaboration, your own leadership must be open to changing the status quo.

Sometimes, nonprofits place a higher value on internal as opposed to external innovation. I urge you to reject the pride that sides with a "not invented here" bias. Innovation is innovation, whether it's found inside or outside your nonprofit. It may even make sense for larger nonprofits to create the role of "Chief Innovation Officer" with a budget to scan the horizon for new ideas, talent, or organizations and propose ways to stay current as part of regular leadership team meetings. Smaller nonprofits can lean into what is coming out from the larger ones.

Innovating ideas

Many nonprofits focus successfully on finding new or better client services. This is a great way to encourage innovation. Breakthrough Urban Ministries, a nonprofit serving the community of East Garfield Park in Chicago, is a wonderful example of growth and innovation based on expanding client services.

Breakthrough provides people affected by poverty with education, workforce development, housing, health and wellness, violence prevention, and spiritual formation.[47] Twenty-five years ago, Arloa Sutter, the founder of Breakthrough, began by simply offering coffee to the homeless people gathered in the foyer of her church. Since then, she and her team have grown into a multimillion-dollar organization with educational programs for children as well as adults.

Breakthrough is a model of innovation in the city of Chicago. I'm proud to say that our son, Steve, volunteers as a member of its young professionals board. A key to Breakthrough's innovation is its curiosity about what more it can do for its clients. It keeps asking how it can better solve the problems facing its community with relentless positivity. In the for-profit world, this is generally called finding solutions to customer needs. Whether it be clients or customers, the question is the same: *"What can we do to serve you better?"* The answer leads to innovation.

A twin question that stimulates innovation is: *"How can we serve you better?"* Nonprofits can innovate similar to for-profit companies by finding new and better ways of delivering core services and creating efficiencies in supply chains. Many good examples of this can be seen in nonprofits with international connections and clients.

For example, World Relief is innovating by sending teams of experts from developed countries to train local leaders in developing countries to find, gather, and deploy local resources to combat local problems. By teaching leadership principles and economics to local leaders, World Relief empowers local leaders to make the improvements themselves rather than performing the work and then leaving. Local leaders are mentored in leadership and creating local banks. Programs that are created and led by trained local leaders show increased sustainability on both sides of the equation and drive self-sufficiency.

Imitating the best practices of other nonprofits

They say that imitation is the highest form of flattery. In my view, imitating or adapting a great idea or practice found elsewhere is smart. According to Sam Walton's book *Made in America*, Wal-Mart was built almost entirely off other retailers' good ideas. "Most everything I've done I've copied from someone else," Walton writes. One of Walton's first jobs in retail was running a franchise for Ben Franklin, a chain of discount stores.[48]

While he was running the Ben Franklin store, Walton often visited his competition across the street. "What really drove Sam was that competition across the street—John Dunham over at the Sterling Store," Walton's wife, Helen Walton, recalled in the book. "Sam was always over there checking on John. Always. Looking at his prices, looking at his displays, looking at what was going on." Later on, when Walton built the first predecessor to Wal-Mart in Bentonville, Arkansas, he copied everything from Ben Franklin—from the accounting system to shelving," reports Hayley Peterson for *Business Insider*.[49]

It should be noted here, however, that imitation is not on the same level as true innovation, which is defined by its originality. But imitation might keep a nonprofit from falling too far behind, or lead to true innovation based on an outside idea that sparks a new internal one. And, naturally, legal compliance with copyright, trademark, or trade secret must be observed. Sometimes a license can be secured for a protected interest. There is no harm in asking.

Using the internet to poll a wider audience and access thought leaders

Nonprofits are also great at using crowd sourcing to gather ideas that spur innovation. Some run contests and give prizes away for the best ideas about how to solve a specific problem. Some access a bigger audience by conducting surveys about options being considered for growth. Some create campaigns for supporters and donors to vote for or donate to new initiatives. Inviting more voices into the conversation can be informative and fun.

Similarly, follow applicable trends on social media; find which social networks early adopters are active on. Many of these early adopters are willing to respond to questions or connect you with someone else with more expertise. While there's an endless stream of online content today (and much of it is unhelpful), there is also the joy of finding great new content posted by new thought leaders and innovators, free to read or listen to. It just makes sense to take the time to search every now and again on topics that relate to growth and innovation in your area of service.

Making something old new again

Here's another easy-to-implement idea: Pearl Zhu, writing for Innovation Management, suggests going back in time and revamping an old idea into a new format. It suggests "looking back at methods and services that were used in your sector years ago but have now fallen out of use. Can you bring one back in a new updated form? It has been said that Speed Dating is really a relaunch of a Victorian dance format where ladies had cards marked with appointments."[50]

James Clear writes on Entrepreneur.com: "the most creative innovations are often new combinations of old ideas. Innovative thinkers don't create, they connect. Furthermore, the most effective way to make progress is usually by making a one percent improvement to what already works rather than breaking down the whole system and starting over. Iterate, don't originate." A great example of this is the Instant Pot, a blockbuster product which is an improved version of the old-fashioned pressure cooker.[51]

Building continuous refinement and improvement into your nonprofit has another competitive advantage: since these tend not to be visible to the competition, they're hard to borrow. Big innovations like new services, products, and locations are easy to see and hence imitate. What successful practice, product, or program can you reinvigorate and reintroduce by adding a modern twist?

Viewing failure as progress

Inside every innovative idea is the potential, maybe even the probability, of failure. Leaders who desire innovation from their coworkers create cultures that counteract the fear of failure in a way that is meaningful to the dreamers. In some highly innovative cultures like Google, failure is not only expected and accepted as normal, but celebrated because it means that someone is thinking and trying. Failure is the unavoidable precursor to ultimately achieving success. Normalizing failure has the added benefit of keeping your innovators with you rather than leaving and start something new somewhere else.

My good friends, Carl Erickson and his wife Mary O'Neill, have built a successful and innovative software company in Michigan. He often says that at Atomic Object, everything is an experiment. Some go on to become regular practices, offerings, or policies, and some disappear. By calling everything an experiment, his company avoids the trap of perfecting before launching. It also spares delicate egos and makes it easier to throw in the towel when the facts suggest it. Learning from the experiments that don't survive is icing on the cake at Atomic.

Summary of Core Points

- Innovation blindness is a threat because a failure to adapt to change puts the nonprofit's sustainability at risk.

- Experts have identified two reasons companies fail at innovation: only doing more of the same thing, or only doing what's new. Companies that find the balance between the two are not only rare, but also highly rewarded.

- The most successful nonprofits can be the most susceptible to innovation blindness; success breeds arrogance and complacency.

- You must first believe that your nonprofit can become outdated and then commit resources to innovation practices.

- Look for innovative ideas and practices from newer professionals.

- Prepare for the unexpected financial downturn.

- Eliminate any "not invented here" bias and look for opportunities to acquire or legally copy the best practices of other nonprofits.

- Seek information from stakeholders and clients about the effectiveness of current practices and programs.

- Take something old and make it new again with a modern application or improvement.

- View failure as progress.

Coming Up Next

It's a tricky business to balance your nonprofit's excellent track record with effective innovation for the future, and it requires organizational calm so people can think and dream. This is precisely why, in the next chapter, you'll learn some ways to stay out of distracting and disruptive spotlights. Reputational damage can last a long time. Find out how to prevent costly and time-consuming mistakes that attract that dreaded and unwanted headline.

CHAPTER 9

Step 9: Protect Your Reputation

> *"Don't wait until you're in a crisis*
> *to come up with a crisis plan."*
>
> — Phil McGraw

> *"In a crisis, don't hide behind anything or*
> *anybody. They're going to find you anyway."*
>
> — Bear Bryant

When I wake up in the morning and read another scandalous headline about a nonprofit, I picture a boat suddenly taking on water in rough seas. The boat's captain and crew must act quickly to stop the water coming in, or the boat will lose buoyancy and sink. When facts emerge that hurt a nonprofit's reputation, leadership needs to act fast to restore public trust and keep the nonprofit from sinking under waves of rapid and repetitive negative publicity. But it has to take the *right* action. This chapter is designed to share key lessons I've learned while being in the center of some of these storms.

I'll confess, I learned most of the lessons in this chapter the hard way. I learned them during some of the toughest times in my nonprofit service. They've usually started with notification about a mistake or misconduct by someone on the internal team.

This news then triggers the need to spend a lot of immediate time figuring out what happened and deciding what to do next. This activity, of course, also costs money that was not earmarked for crisis control. To be honest, my experience is that the results of all the time, work, and the money spent are generally mixed at best. It's really hard to put the toothpaste back into the tube. The truth is that not all reputational damage can be fully mitigated. Most of these situations are a little like stepping on an IED. You can survive, but still lose a limb.

The causes of scandal are so varied that it's nearly impossible to completely prevent all of them from happening. The circumstances that threaten the reputation of a nonprofit usually catch a board or leadership team off guard. Why? Because mistakes by definition are unintentional, and bad acts are not done out in the open. Embezzlers don't announce that they're cooking the books, and harassers don't broadcast their sleazy come-ons. It's hard to see the negative headlines coming. That's why it's so important, as much as possible, to build prevention into management systems.

It is my belief that too few nonprofits have good crisis management plans at the ready because of denial. We all want to believe we can beat the odds, or that no one in our circles will make a giant mistake or misbehave. I'm hoping that this chapter will help you prepare a great plan *that you will never need to use.*

Case Study #7: United Way

United Way is a nationwide umbrella group for thousands of local United Way organizations that fund social and human service projects. In the early 90s, the 22-year president and CEO of United Way of America, William Aramony, was convicted on 25 felony counts and sentenced to seven years in prison for fraudulently diverting $1.2 million of the charity's money to benefit himself and his friends. Before the scandal broke, Aramony was widely respected as one of the most influential nonprofit leaders of his time. He even had a hand in creating many of the rules under which charities operate today.[52]

The fallout from the scandal was huge. Many United Way affiliates opted out of the partnership umbrella, and fundraising dropped nationwide. The *Los Angeles Times* reported that a year after the scandal, United Way trimmed its budget from $30 million to $21 million.[53]

Internally, United Way changed how it was governed so that this kind of malfeasance could never happen again. Then it began the long process of rebuilding trust with its partners. Thankfully, United

Way *has* recovered and now has a four-star rating with Charity Navigator, a nonprofit watchdog group. In January 2020, United Way of Metropolitan Dallas received a $10 million legacy gift from the family of board member Mary Anne Sammons Cree, one of the largest gifts ever for that area.

In my experience, when mistakes or misconduct that can cause reputational damage are discovered, a few things immediately occur. Initially the executive director, president, or board chair will make sure the board is briefed with whatever facts are known. A public response is quickly developed for reporters and stakeholders who need to be informed. Usually an attorney for the nonprofit will review applicable insurance policies, policies, handbooks, or employment contracts.

When a scandal involves finances, it is not unusual for a bank, an auditor, or investors to get involved. One thing is for sure: none of these activities were remotely on anyone's mind last week. With a sense of disbelief, the nonprofit leaders privately think, *"How can this be happening to us?"*

Recommended action steps

What can we learn from watching the actions taken by United Way when caught in this unfortunate situation?

Here's some good news. While reputational damage can come from many sources, many of the principles for handling the problems are straightforward. Here's one basic construct to use if your organization is facing a scenario that may cause reputational damage.

1. Identify who will take point leadership

Once the damage to reputation starts, it's important to identify a person or team with the best crisis management skills within the organization. This move will help curb excessive internal indecision and dissension about what to do. The identity of that person might be a surprise.

Ideally, those with top titles are also the best people for this job. But if they're not, another option is to create a temporary task force led by a proven crisis manager. One litmus test is to observe in whose direction heads turn for leadership when the heat is on. I have seen people rise up who go unnoticed when operations are smooth. This is especially true in board circles where officer titles normally follow seniority.

Here's a case in point. Several years ago, the founder of a high-profile nonprofit resigned amidst public accusations of harassment and abuse. The entire board of the organization also resigned under public pressure. A new board was formed, but it wisely deferred to a group of outside experts to investigate and make recommendations about how to handle the accusations. The new board recognized that while they held authoritative positions, a better result might be achieved by delegating to others with greater experience in the matters at hand.

Let me tell you a little family story that also illustrates the point on a smaller scale. Sometimes the most competent crisis manager is the one with the most specific training. Not long ago, my 89-year-old father-in-law got a small cut on his leg as the result of a minor mishap at his home. He and my mother-in-law thought nothing of it, but it was harboring a secret infection.

Not knowing any of this, my husband and I offered them a quick visit with their grandson, a family medicine resident at the local hospital. While in the lobby, my father-in-law suddenly became feverish and sick to his stomach. Right at that moment, their grandson walked out in his white coat and immediately saw that his grandpa was in trouble. There was a split-second nonverbal exchange between our son and me. He shot me that, *"What's going on here, Mom?"* look, expecting some answers. But not knowing about the cut, I gave him a bewildered face. Immediately, his medical training kicked in.

Speaking gently and reassuringly to his grandpa, he slowly unwound his stethoscope and began to take his grandpa's vitals. The loving grandson turned into the doctor on call. Happily, my father-in-law got better during his week in the hospital. He also really enjoyed his celebrity status as Dr. Dan's grandpa. The rest of us were very glad to defer to the most trained person in the room in the crunch moment, even if he was also the youngest.

2. Empower a trustworthy crisis team

It's important that the chosen crisis manager or task force have the requisite authority to put out the fire. That authority needs to mirror the responsibility that will be undertaken. It's vital that people inside and outside the organization view this person or team as wise, experienced, and accountable. This is key to rebuilding damaged trust.

I have seen organizations stumble on this point. In an effort to try to control the outcome, they'll pick people who are not perceived as impartial and dedicated to discovering and telling the truth. This is a mistake because it hinders the rebuilding of trust and the ultimate credibility of the outcome.

Early missteps in the choice of crisis leadership and in the initial public statements have consequences that can last a long time and complicate restoration. Don't underestimate the problem. In this day and age of Twitter and other social media outlets, a few angry voices can gain a lot of traction. One way to buy a bit more response time is to simply say initially, "We are committed to truth and transparency and will be coming forward with more information soon."

3. Remove management of the crisis from the day-to-day nonprofit operations

Once the crisis management team is formed, it can be announced to staff and supporters. This action helps separate the crisis management activity from the day-to-day activities of the nonprofit. This separation prevents the good work of the nonprofit from being swallowed up by the crisis. It will also assure those not directly involved in its solution that the problem is being competently addressed, and allow them to detach from it as much as they can. Giving regular updates on the crisis team's progress will reduce the stress on the rank and file that knows something is going on but cannot directly impact the outcome.

4. Commit to finding and telling the truth

The team can then move to developing a high-integrity, quality investigation to get at the truth, or as much of it as can ever be known. Because serious and credible questions have been raised about the trustworthiness of the nonprofit, it's imperative to conduct a proper investigation to protect its reputation. A quality investigation protects the person or persons accused of mistakes or misconduct from speculation as well. Here is another common point of misstep: engaging in an investigation that will not hold up to public scrutiny and your critics. If the house is on fire, you need to know *for certain* if it was caused by faulty wiring or kids playing with matches.

What if the facts giving rise to the reputational damage turn out to be entirely false? Great! A quality investigation can serve to put to rest false facts better than repeated denials or ignoring the issues. Failure to conduct a genuine and effective investigation, however, subjects the nonprofit to ongoing and persistent questions about its trustworthiness and credibility—the lifeblood of sustainable success.

5. Prioritize fiduciary duty

A board must have undivided loyal to the best interests of the nonprofit. This is part of its fiduciary duty to the organization. Sometimes this means the person at the center of the controversy may be asked to cooperate with an investigation so the cloud of distrust can be removed from the nonprofit's mission as well as from him or her. Reluctance to let a fair process fully play out is a red flag. It's a mistake to think that covering up wrongdoing will protect a nonprofit.

Here is a well-known case in point. In 2011, a long-term and celebrated Pennsylvania State University football coach, Gerald A. Sandusky, was criminally charged with sexual abuse of minors. He was convicted of 45 counts and sentenced to jail. Moreover, former Penn State President Graham Spanier, 68, was sentenced to four to 12 months. Former Penn State Athletic Director Tim Curley, 63, received a sentence of seven to 23 months, with three in jail. Former Vice President Gary Schultz, 67, was given six to 23 months, with two months behind bars. All pleaded guilty to child endangerment.

According to the *Star Tribune*, Spanier said he regretted that "I did not intervene more forcefully." Schultz said, "It really sickens me to think I might have played a part in children being hurt."

The case against them hinged on coaching assistant Mike McQueary's claim that he witnessed Sandusky—a retired member of the coaching staff who ran a charity for youngsters—molesting a boy in the team showers in 2001. Prosecutors said that after McQueary recounted what he saw, the three administrators decided not to report it to authorities. They thought they were protecting the university's reputation, but the exact opposite was true.[54]

Case study #8: The Freeh report, a model for how to conduct a credible and effective investigation

What are the features of a successful investigation? Let's look at the one conducted for Penn State by Special Investigative Counsel Louis Freeh and his team.

- To start, *impartial factfinders* are essential to the viability of any process that aims for acceptance of its findings by a majority of those who are concerned about the allegations. It's best to select factfinders that everyone agrees are fair, objective, and qualified.

- In the Penn State case, the university board appointed an independent special investigations task force, which produced what is now called the Freeh report. This report is a good blueprint for how independent investigations should be conducted.

- The process should include *an impartial and equal opportunity for the offended parties to be heard* and express their grievances. This will take time, but it's time well spent. Trust can be broken if information is leaked from confidential meetings, so special care should be taken to avoid it.

- When the facts have been gathered, *the factfinders should make a response to the complaints*. Sometimes this is a conclusion, and sometimes it's a recommendation based on all the facts.

- Any response should include *a clear statement of all the facts* leading to the determination. This clear and complete statement explaining why the decision was made in the way it was, will at the very least help those who do not agree with the ultimate decision have confidence that a fair process was followed.

- We'll talk more in a moment about how and to whom this communication should be made, because it's not a one-size-fits-all answer. The key, however, is that *all parties should feel satisfaction with the quality and fairness of the process* even if, at the end of the day, they're not satisfied with the outcome itself.

- It should be noted that even the fairest processes do not guarantee that everyone will be one hundred percent happy with the result. But an impeccable process will greatly assist the nonprofit in emerging from the reputational damage.

- Sadly, processes like this cost considerable money and time. However, both are well spent if trust in the organization is ultimately preserved or restored. Proper process has the added benefit of keeping the matter from becoming so entrenched and alive that restoring trust is potentially unattainable.

Communicating effectively in a crisis

"It has been said that nothing dispels a lie faster than the truth; nothing exposes the counterfeit faster than the genuine."

— R.C. Sproul

A strong lesson from the Penn State scandal is that covering up wrongdoing is not a winning strategy for protecting or restoring reputation. Every organization, when confronted with facts that threaten its reputation, should commit to responsibly investigate and tell the truth to those with a right to know. This is the best and possibly the only way to protect or restore public trust. Making no response, or making an inadequate response, leaves the door open for a landslide of negative speculation, additional reputational damage, and can prevent the nonprofit from leaving the crisis behind.

Regular and accurate updates throughout the process are necessary to tamp down negative and often untrue speculation. Updates help everyone stay informed and encouraged during the investigation. Outside communications teams can also help to bring consistency and competence to private and public communications because internal communication teams, though highly skilled at managing normal communications for the nonprofit, may be ill prepared to handle crisis communications.

A helpful principle I learned along the way is to "tell the whole truth to whom the whole truth is due." This is not easy to achieve by any standard. On one hand, leadership that underreports runs the risk that the controversy will never be put to rest due to too many unanswered public questions. On the other hand, overreporting can spread the problem like oil on water and create more reputational damage with those who did not need to be informed.

Match communication to exposure

The principle "tell the whole truth to whom the whole truth is due" means that the release of information should match or mirror, as much as possible, the level of exposure that the allegations have reached. It's a bit like choosing the bandage that best fits the size of the wound. For example, if the controversy has reached national or international levels, the findings of an impartial process should cover that same amount of territory. Likewise, if the controversy is known only by a smaller audience, aim for coverage of that audience.

Sometimes good organizations deal with a scandal correctly, but fail to adequately disclose the findings of an impartial investigation to a wide enough audience. With the reach of the internet, local nonprofits sometimes have a much wider reputation and impact than they realize. That larger audience is also entitled to a full report if not telling them will negatively impact the nonprofit's mission. To visit the medical analogy once again, failure to address all impacted parties is like vaccinating one person when an entire village has been exposed to the disease.

At the end of the day, all crisis communication involves a measure of risk. My friend Bob Ferguson, founder of the Hawksbill Group, a public relations firm in Washington, D.C., says that every communication made during a crisis has the potential to help or hurt the organization.[55] That's why public relations professionals like Bob are so helpful. They can use their experience to predict how your crisis communication plan will address the needs based on how similar plans have addressed them in other crisis scenarios. After evaluating the ability of your internal communications team to handle crisis communications, you can decide whether to engage outside help for consultation.

Restoring a nonprofit's reputation after it's been damaged in the public's mind isn't a slam dunk, and harder to do under pressure.

This is why it's so important to have a good crisis communication plan in place. Saying too little—or in some cases, saying too much—can create the need to spend more time and money than was originally necessary. Remember: in the presence of a communication vacuum, people usually draw the worst conclusions about the nonprofit and its leadership.

Again, a good crisis communication plan starts with an honest pledge to investigate and take corrective action if something is found to be amiss. The nonprofit must ensure the public understands their commitment to do the right thing no matter what. Half measures generally will not suffice to put the organization back on firm footing. As with an infection, failure to take the whole course of antibiotics can lead to relapse and delay a full recovery.

Prevention tips

Here's an astute observation from an expert. Organizations that fall prey to disrepute have usually ignored the warning signs marking the road to trouble. Mark De Moss, the retired founder of the De Moss Public Relations firm in Atlanta, says: "Most PR problems aren't really PR problems; they're *management* problems that have become *public*."

Mark is right, just judging by the number of times various organizations' internal employee emails have revealed insider knowledge of damaging problems before they became public. A recent example of this are the Boeing pilot emails discussing problems with the 737 Max airplane, two of which crashed and caused significant loss of life. The damage to Boeing's reputation, while secondary to the personal tragedy, was immense.

What kinds of things can you do now to decrease the chances that you'll need a crisis management plan?

1. First, read all the chapters of this book and use them as a way to talk about the health and preparedness of your people, operations, and practices.

2. Create a culture of openness that encourages people to bring to light things they think put the organization at risk.

3. Be committed to best business practices throughout your nonprofit that decrease the chances of hidden bad acts.

Summary of Core Points

- Events that publicly damage a nonprofit's reputation are unusual, but the cost can be high and prolonged.

- It pays to have a crisis management plan in advance of a sudden negative event.

- Commit to finding and telling the truth.

- Empower a high-integrity crisis team. This team is not always found in those with the most senior titles.

- Conduct a process that's above reproach around the inflammatory issues. It should include a thorough investigation, impartial factfinders and decision-makers, and ample communication to stakeholders.

- Understand that coverups never succeed in protecting an organization's reputation.

- Create a culture of openness and penalty-free reporting so internal management problems don't become pubic.

- Institute best business practices to decrease the potential for secret bad acts.

Coming Up Next

The next chapter looks at how sustainability is threatened when organizations fail to leverage a huge nonprofit advantage: deploying volunteers. Increased costs of operation and decreased community influence are just two of the consequences of neglecting this enormous nonprofit advantage. Finding, organizing, training, and rewarding volunteers is an art. While the payoffs for including volunteers are big, some nonprofits still shy away from cracking the code on this advantage. Read on to find out why and what can be done to create systems and cultures that all volunteers can thrive in and upon which the nonprofit can grow.

CHAPTER 10

Step 10: Attract and Retain Excellent Volunteers

"People are yearning to be asked to use the full measure of their potential for something they care about."

— Dan Pallotta, author and founder,
Charity Defense Council

"Volunteers will get you through times of no money better than money will get you through times of no volunteers."

— Ken Wyman, Fundraising & Advocacy Counsultant

Time is money

Competition for volunteers is stiff, and successful nonprofits who are good at attracting, managing, and retaining them get more done. Nonprofits without a solid volunteer base pay higher labor costs, which decreases the amount of good they can do. Like it or not, in the nonprofit world, time is money.

A lack of volunteers also leads to lower contact with the greater community, resulting in fewer donations and less outside expertise contributing to the needs of the nonprofit. Nonprofits that fail to leverage the advantages volunteers offer is like heating a home with fuel oil versus solar power. Fuel oil is more expensive, less efficient, and a lot more wasteful of limited resources. This chapter explains how to find great volunteers and keep them coming back.

Case Study #9: Community Threads

I'm passionate about volunteer engagement because I saw what they could do at Community Threads, a 25,000-square-foot nonprofit resale shop in Arlington Heights, Illinois that I founded in 2011. Three hundred volunteers showed up to work every month and were primarily responsible for producing a million dollars in gross revenue a year, 35-40% of which was profit. From that profit, over three million in grants has been awarded to other charities for poverty relief and scholarships for kids. Volunteers served at every level, from maintenance to management.

Volunteers were included on the leadership, visual merchandising, pricing, customer service, and donation processing team. Over 95% of the cashiers were also volunteers. At Community Threads, volunteers managed large departments and were the store's best advocates, recruiters, donors, and shoppers. Paid personnel were limited to fifteen positions, including nine that were part time for a store open to the public sixty-five hours a week. This case study is a powerful example of how volunteers can help nonprofits lower costs and increase community engagement.[56]

On a national level, volunteerism in the United States is at record levels. The 2018 *Volunteering in America* report found that 77.34 million adults (30.3%) volunteered through an organization last year. Altogether, Americans volunteered nearly 6.9 billion hours, worth an estimated $167 billion in economic value. In addition, one in three volunteers raises funds for nonprofits (36%). This is a huge incentive for your nonprofit to invest in volunteer recruitment, management, and retention. Volunteers represent a tremendous opportunity to grow your nonprofit and offer exceptional volunteering experiences in your area.[57]

Believe in the power of volunteers

Finding and retaining great volunteers starts with a belief in the value of volunteers. While this may seem obvious, I can tell you that a number of my clients mistakenly started out thinking that volunteer labor wasn't worth the leadership effort and liability risks. Many leaders, even unknowingly, prefer to work with paid staff because volunteers often require more training and are motivated by leadership influence as opposed to a paycheck.

It is true that volunteers can sometimes be less reliable or behind on technology and best workplace practices. They require a different kind of leadership model that compensates for these areas and places volunteers in positions that can accommodate the typical fluctuations inherent in a volunteer workforce. My own experience in leading hundreds of volunteers, however, affirms that volunteer engagement, when done well, propels nonprofit objectives.

In order to successfully incorporate volunteers, staff members need to be trained in how to lead them. Volunteers come with many skillsets and can relieve the burden on busy staff. One mental hurdle to overcome is the temptation to think, "I [staff member] can do this better and faster myself rather than take time to train a volunteer." This will always be true. It is also the fast track to burnout and prioritizes the urgent over the important.

Some people are more adept at volunteer engagement than others. That said, for volunteer engagement to really thrive, paid staff must appreciate the benefit that volunteers bring to the organization. I once heard one of my employees exclaim, "I hate working with volunteers!" after a particularly frustrating exchange with a volunteer newcomer. It turned out that this employee was more effective in a bookkeeping position working with numbers rather than people and she was invaluable there. She also appreciated very much the way volunteer service positively impacted those numbers!

If your nonprofit can be enhanced through volunteers, it's important to make volunteer recruitment and retention the responsibility of a talented leader. This leader will become the volunteer champion, implement the volunteer engagement plan, and oversee the integration of volunteers into the life of the nonprofit. They will also adapt whatever online volunteer management tool is selected.

Beyond adding leadership horsepower to the equation, constructing a welcoming and respectful environment for your volunteers is key to recruiting and retaining them. Volunteers who feel respected stay and recruit others. Respect is defined as providing volunteers with excellent places to serve, supportive supervisors, uncluttered workspaces, clean air, good lighting, adequate training, and well-organized operations.

For example, many volunteers have regular jobs or family responsibilities during the day. Respecting their work and family lives when creating opportunities for them to serve signals that they are respected and seen. One way to do this is to schedule key meetings at times that work for them.

Give to get

When working with volunteers, it pays to keep in mind the WIFM—"what's in it for me"—principle. Many nonprofits try to recruit volunteers mainly by telling them what volunteers can do for the nonprofit or stressing how much the nonprofit needs them.

Certainly, volunteers will be attracted to the needs you're trying to meet, so this should always be a part of the invitation to serve.

But it's important to balance the message of need with the message of what volunteering can do for the volunteer. They certainly will want to know that their work is meaningful and serving an important purpose. But they will love being part of a healthy community where they will be trained, grow, and receive recognition.

The reward principle applies to volunteer engagement as much as in the workforce, and perhaps more so because volunteers don't receive the reward of a regular paycheck. Finding a win-win between the nonprofit and the volunteer is central to great volunteer recruitment and retention. Certainly, altruism is at the heart of volunteerism, but smart nonprofit leaders know to offer something valuable to their volunteers in gratefulness for their valuable contributions.

Volunteer management fundamentals

Respect also entails creating an environment where volunteers understand what's expected of them. Most people know that goals are achieved through effective management of people, resources, and time. When they're part of a paid workforce, they recognize that reliability, responsibility-taking, and time management are necessary components to getting hired and being promoted. However, volunteers can be tempted to think that not being paid means that these important workplace attributes are suspended. That's why setting expectations for each volunteer position is so important.

Volunteers need to have the choice about which expectations they wish to meet. No one can or should force a volunteer into an activity which has a higher expectation of performance than they're willing to give. Volunteers can be given opportunities at lower levels of performance expectations as well as higher levels of performance expectations.

For volunteers to make clear choices, they need to accurately understand what's expected so no one gets hurt feelings or inadvertently fails. Many disappointments can be avoided by making sure that volunteers are given a clear understanding of the expectations associated with volunteer service. My experience is that most people want to fulfill their commitments.

Illustrating this practice at Community Threads, we welcomed untrained "drop-in" volunteers who didn't want to be scheduled for a regular three-hour service time slot. They were given tasks that didn't require much training, and while important, did not reflect much authority or ongoing responsibility. Because the staff was committed to creating the best volunteer experience possible for each volunteer, the store required drop-in volunteers to return the courtesy with a two-hour minimum service time.

Empower volunteers according to their commitment level

Here's an example of a volunteer with high-level performance expectations. A good friend of mine is a retired finance executive of a Fortune 500 company and served as a volunteer Interim CFO at a $250-million nonprofit for over a year. Even though he was volunteering, his skillset and work ethic were no different than when he was being highly paid. What a boon for this nonprofit! Many retired professionals come with seasoned skillsets that can help a nonprofit far beyond its ability to hire people with that experience. He went on to be selected as the president of his undergraduate alma mater.

A retired dentist friend of mine volunteers weekly at a free clinic for the underserved through his church. Other volunteers know how to fundraise, develop and market products, create strategic plans, and engage in community relations or legislative affairs. Some have legal or medical training. The areas of expertise where volunteers can serve are endless. Attracting volunteers who thrive at this level will depend on how good *you* are—not how good they are.

Maintain a pleasant and safe work environment

For any organization to work efficiently, it's important that all contributors, whether paid or unpaid, show up for commitments on time, comply with workplace standards, and follow leadership direction. It can be helpful to ask volunteers to sign commitment cards or provide a welcome packet that explains community standards and expectations. It's a bit counter-intuitive, but most people appreciate being called to their best.

Fear of losing volunteers is one motivation for allowing them to exceed boundaries or behave badly. But tolerance of bad habits can boomerang and discourage the best volunteers. No one wants to work in an environment where incivility, gossip, slacking, and negativity are the norm. No one should feel that their feelings, identity, and moral compasses are being violated. Good conflict resolution forums and practices offer volunteers a way to safely express dissatisfaction or report things that need to be addressed. Of course, volunteers will know if you really care about them or not. Some ideas below help put that care into action.

Invest in volunteer training and management

My experience is that volunteers who care about the nonprofit's mission want to be good at what they do. They fear making mistakes. Good-hearted people want to be helpful in ways that have the greatest impact. They also enjoy learning new skillsets and achieving mastery over a new task. Here's where the development of clear training materials and practice exercises can help attract and retain volunteers who may initially feel unqualified to serve. Because it takes time to create great training presentations, consider using some proven online resources.

According to VolunteerHub, volunteer training can be categorized into three types: basic nonprofit education, organization-based training, and role-specific training. A few of the most common training formats are video, readings, lecture-style, and audio format. Online training programs are also an appealing, viable option for some nonprofit organizations who want to reach volunteers all over the world or provide a convenient training option to supporters. Providing volunteers with options for how they can complete their training increases the likelihood of effectively delivering the information and promoting learnability.[58]

Like Volunteer Hub, Volgistics is a good, affordable volunteer management system. Volgistics enables nonprofits to schedule, communicate with, and train volunteers online. Volunteer management systems like these also gather valuable data about the volunteers that assists in recruitment, training, and retention.[59]

Eleven places to find great volunteers

Fortunately, with so many people interested in volunteering, there are a lot of great ways to connect with them. Here are some that have worked well for me.

1. Create a winsome volunteer profile to post on established volunteer websites like volunteermatch.com, nonprofitvillage.com, goodsurfing.org, All for Good, Catchafire, iVolunteer, or DonorsChoose. Inquiries about your organization will begin to flow. You can then begin a

conversation with people about what it means to volunteer for your nonprofit.

2. Look online for the names of companies that run employee volunteer programs and fairs. Some of these companies, like Allstate and Starbucks, also give financial assistance to nonprofits that accept their employees as volunteers.

3. Contact local high schools and colleges about their requirements for student community service hours. Many schools require their students to volunteer at local nonprofits in order to graduate or be part of an honors program. They normally have an approved nonprofits list for students to investigate. Once you make that connection, student word of mouth can help keep the connection going if they enjoyed their experience.

4. Ask your current volunteers to bring a friend with them. Add incentives to bring along a volunteer friend through some kind of recognition, service discount, or an occasional small gift card.

5. Use social media to get the word out that your nonprofit is accepting volunteers. Use your email database, Instagram account, YouTube, or Twitter to make a call for volunteers and help create a buzz with people seeking opportunities.

6. Seek out court-connected programs for people who are ordered to perform community service for minor offenses. Your nonprofit can set criteria for people who are eligible

to serve at your nonprofit. This may require some reporting back to the court services, but it's generally not cumbersome and worth the extra paperwork.

7. Seek out retirement centers that will allow your nonprofit to post volunteer opportunities for its visitors.

8. Contact churches and other places of worship and offer their members volunteer opportunities.

9. Attend volunteer fairs organized by the local chambers of commerce or local government to highlight volunteer opportunities. Nonprofits typically hand out a small memento such as a pen or a magnet at these fairs to help those who stop by remember where to call.

10. Consider placing an advertisement in the local newspaper. They normally offer an online component, too.

11. Write and send a press release to the local online and print news sources featuring a volunteer interest story.

Gratitude: the engine of joy

We all need encouragement to keep going. Tell your volunteers repeatedly and sincerely that they're doing a great job, that they're making a difference, and that they're good people. It will give them joy.

One way to include volunteers in a meaningful way that deepens their connection with the nonprofit is to share company data that reflects how the nonprofit is doing against goals, and how their efforts are helping. Sharing appropriate inside information with volunteers provides a direct link between what they're doing and the achievement of organizational goals. This practice made everyone feel trusted and invested as an owner.

Another meaningful way of thanking volunteers is a celebration outside work time, where individual volunteer service is highlighted and rewarded. Some nonprofits set up online communities that connect and celebrate their volunteers. Regularly sharing stories of times volunteers have gone above and beyond encourages others to do the same. The highlight of the Community Threads summer volunteer luncheon is when we shared pictures, taken all year long, of the volunteers volunteering.

Celebrating volunteer birthdays and "work anniversaries" is an easy and fun way to thank volunteers. And when a volunteer experiences adversity, helping them out and showing that you care will build a lasting bond. The magic elixir of volunteer success includes providing the chance for fulfilling relationships to grow, showing them respect, and offering meaningful rewards.

Summary of Core Points

- "Volunteers will get you through times of no money better than money will get you through times of no volunteers." —Ken Wyman

- Finding and retaining great volunteers starts with a belief in the value of volunteers.

- To successfully incorporate volunteers, staff members must be trained to lead them well.

- It's important to make volunteer recruitment and retention the responsibility of your best leaders.

- Volunteers who feel respected stay and recruit others. Respect means that volunteers are provided with an excellent place to serve with supportive supervisors, uncluttered workspaces, clean air, good lighting, adequate training, and well-organized operations.

- It's important to balance the message about the nonprofit's needs with a message about what volunteering can do for the volunteer.

- Make sure volunteers are given an upfront, clear understanding of the expectations associated with volunteer service.

- Attracting volunteers who thrive at higher levels will depend on how good *you* are—not how good they are.

169

- Volunteers should be afforded regular forums in which to ask questions or appropriately air grievances.

- The development of clear training materials and exercises can help attract and retain volunteers who may feel unqualified to serve.

- Volunteer management systems can help any nonprofit manage volunteer teams and gather valuable data about them that assists in recruitment and retention.

- Tell your volunteers repeatedly and sincerely that they're doing a great job, that they're making a difference, and that they're good people. It will give them joy.

Coming Up Next

Now let's turn our attention to a real threat that, with careful planning, can be transformed into an advantage. All nonprofits face the inevitable transition of leaders at every level, from volunteers to board members. Loss of important personnel can be a shock to the system. But transitions also offer exciting opportunities for nonprofits to experience something new. Read on about how to avoid transition trauma and replace it with sustainable success.

CHAPTER 11

STEP 11: PREPARE FOR WHAT COMES NEXT

"A leader's lasting value is measured by succession."

— John C. Maxwell

Avoid transition trauma with a great succession plan

Olympic track and field relay team coaches are experts at selecting the right athletes and planning the order in which they will run. They know that some runners are best at managing the curves on the track, some are best at running the long stretches in the middle, and some are superb at anchoring the team and crossing the finish line first.

Each baton handoff must be planned, practiced, and precise. Handoffs during the race are a frequent place for teams to lose precious time or be disqualified. They're also unavoidable. The key is for each team member to trust who's coming before and after them. Why is so much effort expended on team composition, runner placement, and critical handoffs? Because they want to win!

Likewise, a nonprofit that wants to win for the long term must put effort into finding the next leaders and how to conduct the handoffs in the best way possible. Failure to engage in succession planning threatens a nonprofit; without it, your organization can easily become a one-hit wonder. Despite its importance to sustainability, BoardSource reports that *only 27%* of nonprofits have a written succession plan in place.[60]

In one nonprofit I served with, the succession plan consisted of a single sheet of paper, created by the executive director in secret, containing the names of potential successors. He told the board where to find it in the event of his premature demise!

Here are some other reasons succession planning is neglected. Many times, leaders simply do not want to face or plan for their retirement. This is like believing you won't die if you don't have a will. Likewise, boards often neglect succession planning because they're busy dealing with more immediate matters. But this lack of planning makes arriving at the best outcome of any succession process much more difficult.

According to Melanie Lockwood Herman and Erin Gloeckner writing for the Nonprofit Risk Management Center, "The lack of a succession plan opens the door to confusion and turmoil in the board room, infighting on the senior management team, concern on the part of key institutional donors, uncertainty and fear among rank and file staff, reduced productivity, and more. Based on our engagements with dozens of nonprofits and nonprofit boards, the absence of a plan outlining critical steps in the wake of a CEO departure is the #1 risk issue keeping members of nonprofit boards awake at night."[61] The dire and predictable consequences described here combined with the low number of nonprofits reportedly taking any action to prevent them makes the lack of succession planning one of the top twelve nonprofit threats to sustainable success.

Thankfully, there are many good resources and tools for boards and leaders to engage around this issue. One of them, Tom Adams' book *The Nonprofit Leadership Transition and Development Guide*, reminds readers that the purpose of a succession plan is not to select an understudy for your CEO. The purpose is to undertake a planning process that will ensure the health of your nonprofit during and after a leadership change.[62]

Leverage the opportunities that come with leadership transition

Leadership transition presents some good opportunities for nonprofits as well. These transitions can often be marked by celebrations that highlight achievements and remind people of the value and importance of the mission. They're also opportunities to retain top talent who can see future advancement on the horizon. Tom Adams notes that since the only thing we can count on is change, leadership transitions should be anticipated and viewed as wonderful opportunities to grow and transform. Whether a transition occurs due to an unexpected vacancy or the anticipated transition of a long-tenured leader, being deliberative, thoughtful, and having a plan in place can help a nonprofit weather the inevitable challenges of leadership transition.[63]

Another compelling reason for nonprofit leaders to plan for succession is that it's a necessary component of any organization's strategic plan, and vice versa. The two are different but importantly linked. Succession planning and strategic planning both confirm a vision for the business, review goals, and create plans for the achievement of these goals. Succession is often wickedly intertwined with the state of the board's functioning and the enterprise's strategy, too, writes Thomas Gilmore in the *Nonprofit Quarterly Magazine*.[64]

One way to determine where succession planning is needed is for leaders to ask themselves what position, if left unfilled or filled by the wrong person, would cost the organization the most money and forward momentum. The answer to this question will highlight where the nonprofit most needs to engage in succession planning. It's not limited to just the top spot. Don't be surprised if your list includes a key executive assistant.

In fact, succession planning is a great place for internal discussions and activities around how to mentor and groom the next crop of leaders. Studies have shown that internal successors have a higher rate of success than those chosen from the outside because they know and are known by the culture and have proven their commitment to the mission. However, for succession pipelines to work, performance evaluation systems need to be updated, fair, and accurate. Smart leaders create developmental plans for high-potential employees. These plans can include evaluation of their current skills and potential, organizational needs both short and long term, and where skill gaps exist and how to shrink those gaps.[65]

Donors look for sustainability and continuity

Lastly, making time for succession planning is important because transitions normally impact giving critical to nonprofits. Leadership transitions are times of vulnerability for nonprofits. Therefore, it's common for donors to take a "wait and see" approach to new leadership. The loss of a long-tenured leader can make long-tenured donors nervous, especially those who are deeply connected to the departing leader. Succession planning gives the nonprofit an opportunity to include those donor stakeholders in the search process, and offers them valuable information about what the nonprofit is seeking in a new leader.[66]

According to Nick Price, writing for BoardEffect.com, grant-makers also want assurance that the nonprofits they support have solid long-term leadership. Many foundations and grant-making entities offer valuable resources to nonprofit boards on how to develop a succession plan. Philanthropists want nonprofit organizations to succeed, so many of them offer formal board development programs.[67]

When and how to prepare for succession planning

Let's look at some compelling statistics. In a 2013 paper titled, "The Leadership in Leaving," Frances Kunreuther, Phyllis Segal, and Stephanie Clohesy write: "Estimates suggest that up to 75% of U.S. nonprofit leaders are planning to leave their positions in the next five to ten years. With over 1 million nonprofits and philanthropic institutions, the implications of the expected turnover are enormous. By even a modest estimate, a half-million executives may exit their positions over the next 15 years."[68] Moreover, *Philanthropy Journal News* advises that with four million baby boomers retiring each year, the need for a succession plan is a "when" rather than an "if" scenario.[69]

It's safe to say that the time is now to intentionally cultivate the next generation of leaders and plan for succession. The management team could start by identifying or reviewing its strategic goals. Next, identify the core competencies needed to achieve those goals for the future. Following this, assess how many of those competencies are represented in the staff, and which need to be cultivated or found in new hires. Do those core competencies reside in leaders who are likely to transition soon? If so, can an immediate replacement be readily identified?

Case Study #10: Army Strong

Perhaps the best example of an organization that consistently plans for succession is the military. The United States Army has roughly a half million active duty personnel, and another two hundred and fifty thousand civilian employees. Army leadership faces volatile, uncertain, complex, and ambiguous strategic problems, usually during eras of fiscal austerity.

Interestingly, the United States National Security Strategy is described in just four points:

1. The security of the United States, its citizens, and U.S. allies and partners;

2. A strong, innovative, and growing U.S. economy in an open international economic system that promotes opportunity and prosperity;

3. Respect for universal values at home and around the world; and

4. A rules-based international order advanced by U.S. leadership that promotes peace, security, and opportunity through stronger cooperation to meet global challenges.[70]

That kind of clarity allows Army leadership to measure the potential of a future leader by how well they contribute to the achievement of these goals. It's a model and incentive for nonprofit leaders to develop clear goals by which to hire and measure current and future talent.

But what about smaller nonprofits that do not have the staff size to mimic the processes that work for larger nonprofits? Here's a two-step approach. When a nonprofit has a very shallow leadership bench depth, it's smart to split the problem into two plans. The first is an "emergency or interim" plan, and the second is a "steady-state/permanent" plan.

In the emergency plan, the board chair is tapped to do *only* those things that absolutely must be done. These activities are specifically defined with access codes and documented details. Next, the executive committee forms a search committee as soon as possible. That search team can consider both inside and outside candidates. By using the board chair as a temporary executive director, the nonprofit avoids falling into chaos and not having to burden a staff member who may not have the needed skillsets. Then, the more permanent plan can be developed using the guidelines below.

Succession planning precursors

Before launching into succession planning, it's good to consider whether the board of directors has the right mix for hiring the new executive. Competent and well-rounded boards are critical to selecting and empowering senior leaders. It may be that the board must be strengthened before succession planning can be optimally effective.

Blue Avocado, the magazine of the Nonprofit Insurance Alliance, adds these valuable tips: examine the current job profile for the executive director, board members, and senior leaders and ask whether it's still accurate, reasonable, and able to be fulfilled by one person. Enhance the succession process by updating it to reflect the latest strategic goals, number of direct reports, and scope of work.[71]

Of course, salary levels should be reviewed for all positions that are part of the succession plan. It's not unusual to discover that the current executive director's compensation is lower than what a successor will accept, especially if the current leader is a founder. This fact alone might cause a revision of the budget or bring on fundraising activity.

Another good step to take ahead of succession planning is to ascertain whether there are any obvious candidates for the job. In this case, a good succession process should still proceed but could be tailored to make sure the natural successor is truly the best choice, and garner consensus and support for the candidate from all stakeholders.

While selection of a nonprofit's top leader belongs to the board of directors, the best succession process involves a wide range of stakeholders and constituents. The benefit of adding many voices and opinions to the mix is to provide the chosen leader with a broad base of support. Here again, the board can guarantee process satisfaction if not also result satisfaction to all constituents. It doesn't compromise the authority or prerogative of the board to include many voices in the selection and evaluation process.

One final thing to consider for those embarking on a succession planning process is to assess and prepare the organization for the likely income dip that may occur during a search and transition process. The succession plan should account for the cost of the leadership gap between the old and new leaders, the lull that could occur in fundraising, and the possibility that the initial search will fail or take an extended amount of time. In this case, the plan could incorporate an interim strategy.

Fifteen necessary elements of any successful succession plan

Many argue that selecting and managing the chief executive is the *most important* task of the board. Succession planning falls under "duty of care," which is a fiduciary duty of all board directors. Board directors are responsible for ensuring the long-term sustainability of the organization. Recruiting and maintaining effective leadership at the top is a major part of the board's fiduciary responsibilities.[72]

But how does this happen on a practical level, and how can staff leaders assist their boards? From my own experience, and by learning from many good sources, here's a list of necessary elements for a good succession plan.

1. Starting at the top, a successful succession planning process needs the full commitment of both the board and the staff. As the Board Source survey shows, nearly three quarters of all nonprofits do not intentionally engage in succession planning enough to put it in writing.

2. Create or update the nonprofit's strategic plan, including goals and threats that lie ahead. The nonprofit can then objectively determine what leadership qualities and skills are necessary to achieve the goals and defeat the threats.

3. Evaluate where and in what quantity the needed leadership skillsets are currently present in the staff.

4. Create development plans and set target goals for current leaders to acquire needed skillsets or create new positions to add the needed skillsets and build bench strength.

5. In an emergency situation, consider placing an interim leader at the helm for 6-18 months to stabilize the nonprofit while selecting and transitioning to the next permanent leader.

6. Establish a reasonable and realistic timeline for completion of the succession plan.

7. Create a list of the nonprofit's stakeholders and decide who can serve on a succession planning team. The task force is charged with making recommendations to the board, which makes the final selection. Board members should be included on the task force.

8. Create a communication strategy to communicate important updates about the succession planning team's progress to the stakeholders and nonprofit community.

9. Include in the plan leadership development opportunities for staff and board members to increase their leadership skills and enhance the overall leadership expertise within the nonprofit.

10. Consider adding cross-training and internships to the plan to deepen leadership skills and mitigate unexpected staffing challenges.

11. Include in the plan ways to "on board" new employees with mentoring, coaching, and regular feedback.

12. Review, update, or create performance evaluation systems that lead to the objective identification of potential future leaders and eliminate bias and faulty promotions.

13. Include in the succession plan an outline of how the departing leader will be honored and celebrated, as well as how the new leader will be installed and validated.

14. Include in the succession plan how the board and top staff will manage donor relations during any transition process. Consider extra measures that will need to be taken in an emergency or as the result of a contentious departure by the departing leader.

15. Institute a yearly review and an update to the nonprofit's succession plans. Monitor the effectiveness of the employee evaluation plan and satisfaction level of current employees with advancement opportunities.

Balancing the participation of the exiting senior leader is oftentimes an added struggle; a departing leader may not always approach the transition process in a way that benefits the nonprofit. If your exiting leader is tempted to rush the process or ration the information given to the successor, then the scene could be set for a crisis at your nonprofit.[73]

With rare exceptions, the exiting leader is a key player in assuring a pleasant transition to his successor. To manage the risk that your departing leader will rush or be less than generous, ask the departing leader to reflect on the knowledge, processes, and cultural traits possessed by the nonprofit and its personnel that will be beneficial to the successor.[74]

Summary of Core Points

- Leadership transition is inevitable. Therefore, succession planning is essential to organizational sustainability.

- Boards without clarity around the succession process will find themselves scrambling when faced with the unexpected departure of a top leader.

- A lack of planning makes achieving the best outcome in any succession process much more difficult.

- Leadership transitions also present opportunities for nonprofits. They can often be marked by celebrations that highlight achievements and remind people of the value and importance of the mission.

- Succession planning and strategic planning both confirm a vision for the business. Review goals and create plans for the achievement of these goals.

- When a nonprofit has a shallower leadership bench depth, split the problem into two plans. The first is an "emergency or interim" plan, and the second is a "steady-state/permanent" plan.

- It's not unusual to discover that the current executive director's compensation is lower than what a successor will accept, especially if he or she is a founder.

STEP 11: PREPARE FOR WHAT COMES NEXT

- While selection of the top leader belongs to the board of directors, the best succession process involves a wide range of stakeholders and constituents.

- The succession plan should account for the cost of the leadership gap between the old and new leaders.

- Ask the departing CEO to reflect on the nonprofit's knowledge, processes, cultural traits, and its personnel that will be beneficial to the successor.

Coming Up Next

In the gym, weight trainers say it's those final aching repetitions that build your muscles the most. We love the gain from the pain; at the same time, we hate doing them. Likewise, in the next chapter I'm going to stretch you *that last extra bit* in order to give you a valuable advantage over three easily overlooked but important factors to sustainability. And I'll give you some quick-hit ideas about how to implement them as added protection and prevention.

CHAPTER 12

STEP 12: KEEP UP WITH CYBERSECURITY, REGULATORY COMPLIANCE, AND RISK MANAGEMENT

"A leader's lasting value is measured by succession."

— John C. Maxwell

#1 Cybersecurity

"Passwords are like underwear: don't let people see it, change it very often, and you shouldn't share it with strangers."

— Chris Pirillo

STEP 12: KEEP UP WITH CYBERSECURITY, REGULATORY COMPLIANCE, AND RISK MANAGEMENT

For those of us who need a quick definition of cybersecurity, Digital Guardian defines it as the body of technologies, processes, and practices designed to protect networks, devices, programs, and data from attack, damage, or unauthorized access.[75] Whew! While most of us are aware that a threat to our online confidential data exists, few of us are experts at cybersecurity or even know how to best meet the growing threat. Yet the consequences of compromised private data can be huge.

Add to that the weekly headlines about confidential data being stolen from the computer systems of companies, nonprofits, and governments. These thefts are usually attributed to malicious hackers and criminal networks dedicated to stealing, selling, or otherwise misusing the online personal information of employees, customers, and clients.

Cancer Services of East Central Indiana, a small nonprofit in Muncie that provides services to cancer patients, learned a very painful cybersecurity lesson. According to National Public Radio, hackers accessed the nonprofit's server after a staffer inadvertently downloaded malware from an email. The hackers wanted 50 bitcoin, or what was then about $43,000, to return the data and keep it private. The ransom demand email had the subject line: *Cancer Sucks, But We Suck More!*[76]

Michael Wolfe, Chief Technology Officer of Muncie-based software firm Ontario Systems, says there's a lesson here for small nonprofits and businesses. "Stop. Sit down with your board. ... and think through some questions about: What is your IT infrastructure?

Where do you store data? What is your data?" He adds, "I'm sure that there are improvements to be made that could prevent devastation." Hackers don't discriminate, he says, and no matter how small your business or how noble your nonprofit's mission, you could be vulnerable.[77]

Frustratingly, technology alone cannot defeat this threat. In fact, most cybercrimes exploit the biggest weakness in the defensive chain: *human error, such as the employee mentioned above who was tricked into downloading the malware from an email.* The first thing to understand about cybersecurity is that it's constantly changing. Savvy leaders try to keep learning about it, and regularly bring it to the attention of the board who can allocate appropriate resources toward it.

Where can you start protecting your nonprofit from this threat? A quick and easy way to gain more understanding is a free resource called *Cybersecurity for Dummies* by Joseph Carson, CISSP.[78] The short, downloadable PDF provides a basic outline for ways to think about and approach cybersecurity. It will help you create the framework for a discussion with your board and staff around data-related policies and employee online practices.

Carson suggests immediate ways that companies can lessen their susceptibility to common cyber threats typically coming through spam, phishing emails, and social media. The thing to remember is that criminals are looking for certain personal information such as account passwords, social security numbers, and other information related to your credentials and identity. The first line of defense is to deny hackers access to these.

STEP 12: KEEP UP WITH CYBERSECURITY, REGULATORY COMPLIANCE, AND RISK MANAGEMENT

Another good resource to use to develop an information security program is the National Institute of Standards and Technology (NIST) Cybersecurity Framework.[79] The NIST CSF is a set of optional standards, best practices, and recommendations for improving cybersecurity at the organizational level regardless of size, risk profile, or cyber sophistication. NIST wrote the CSF at the behest of President Obama in 2014. The CSF's goal is to create a common language, set of standards, and easily executable series of goals for improving cybersecurity.[80]

Despite the informative materials available on how to protect confidential data, this material is best used to foster personal and company understanding of the overall perils and the fundamentals of cybersecurity rather than being relied upon exclusively for data protection. Nonprofits that collect and store the confidential personal information of clients, employees, volunteers, or donors should consider either hiring staff experts or engaging outside consultants to assess, design, implement, and monitor cybersecurity programs and processes.

Another recommendation is to avoid storing the most sensitive information in the first place. You can't lose what you don't have. For sensitive things that must be stored (social security and driver's license numbers, etc.), consider using paper. Paper is much easier to secure. Avoid storing store credit card numbers. There are plenty of better vendors to outsource to for recurring donations and the like.

Lastly, here are some quick reminders on how to improve your cybersecurity from CoxBLUE.com[81] and AT&T Business.[82] These practices are commonly known, but not always consistently carried out.

1. Back up your data and periodically make sure the data is actually retrievable.

2. Change your passwords.

3. Use a password manager. Tools such as 1Password, LastPass, Dashlane, or Sticky Password help you use unique, secure passwords for every site you need, while also keeping track of them for you. That way, you get the security benefits of changing your password without having to worry about making things hard on your employees. These tools have the added benefit of making sure that someone can get into critical systems if someone else leaves abruptly.

4. Delete unused accounts.

5. Enable two-factor identification.

6. Update your software and run anti-virus scans. For smaller nonprofits, computer repair and protection contracts are available from vendors like the Best Buy Geek Squad that help protect individual computers for smaller fees.

7. Train your staff to identify risks found in emails and on social media.

8. Implement VPNs for all connections. Networks that are protected only by generic security measures are more vulnerable to attack. Implement virtual private network (VPN) connections between office locations and make their use easy—and mandatory—for mobile employees who may connect through public Wi-Fi services.

9. Avoid public Wi-Fi connections and assume they're being monitored.

10. Use a reputable online payment processor.

11. Consider whether using Apple computers over Microsoft Windows makes sense. Macs aren't immune to viruses, but their inherent security is greater. They also aren't as popular with attackers as Windows machines.

Perhaps the most valuable takeaway from this section is that cybersecurity for nonprofits is more than purchasing a prepackaged firewall. To defeat this threat, nonprofits need to be vigilant, assess risks, get advice, and allocate resources. "It takes 20 years to build a reputation and a few minutes of a cyber incident to ruin it," says Stephane Nappo, a global cyber-security expert.

#2 Regulatory Compliance

> *"If you think compliance is expensive—*
> *try non-compliance."*
>
> — Former U.S. Deputy Attorney General Paul McNulty

Let's start with what regulatory compliance is, and what the threat is for nonprofits who fail in this area. Simply stated, regulatory compliance deals with the governmental laws and regulations that nonprofits must obey in order to operate. Conversely, failure to comply with applicable laws can result in the nonprofit being shut down or severely penalized.

Katie Dwyer, writing for Risk & Insurance.com, says that to maintain their tax-exempt status, nonprofits are subject to specific rules set by the IRS. Primarily, nonprofits must demonstrate that they are using funds for a charitable purpose and not for any type of financial or political gain. The IRS prohibits any political activity beyond communicating with legislators as a constituent or responding to government inquiries. Lobbying, for example, is considered inappropriate for a charitable organization and could cost a nonprofit its tax exemption. Even if a nonprofit maintains its status, it could be hit with painful fines.[83]

Furthermore, in the U.S. states and the federal government can dissolve a nonprofit for regulatory noncompliance and levy fines. Fines, the loss of tax-exempt status, and involuntary dissolution are all compelling reasons why failure to maintain regulatory compliance is a top threat for nonprofits. Add to this that there are quite a few ways nonprofits can fall out of regulatory compliance and subject themselves to penalties.

Here are some standard regulatory obligations for nonprofits:

1. Nonprofits must have a purpose that complies with the IRS code.

    Per the IRS, in order to secure charitable tax-exempt status, nonprofits must have a purpose that is "charitable, religious, educational, scientific, literary, testing for public safety, fostering national or international amateur sports competition, and preventing cruelty to children or animals."

    Under IRS code, being charitable includes providing "relief of the poor and distressed or of the underprivileged; advancement of religion; advancement of education or science; erection or maintenance of public buildings, monuments, or works; lessening of the burdens of government; promotion of social welfare."

    This may appear easy to achieve, but I have seen nonprofits struggle with their applications to the IRS. This issue can cost thousands of dollars in legal fees or delay the start of operations.

193

2. Maintain a registered agent who's responsible for receiving legal and tax documents. They must have a physical address (no P.O. boxes) in the state of incorporation and must be available during normal business hours.

3. Nonprofits with $100K in annual contributions or over $250K in assets are required to file a 990 tax form with the IRS each year.[84]

4. File an annual tax return.

5. Maintain a state-level exemption.

6. Refrain from campaigning or lobbying.

7. Maintain proper use of profits.

   While nonprofits can earn profits, any surpluses generated by the entity must remain in the organization, meaning nonprofit organizations cannot distribute profits to individuals. That's the primary difference between for-profit and nonprofit organizations: for-profit organizations can distribute net profits to employees and shareholders, whereas nonprofit status prohibits such activity.

8. Withhold tax from employee paychecks.

   While the entity received tax-exempt status, its employees do not. A nonprofit organization must possess an Employee Identification Number and withhold certain taxes from employee paychecks. A nonprofit organization must also comply with both state and federal employment laws, says Nonprofit Expert.[85] Outsourcing payroll is common practice even for smaller nonprofits.

9. Comply with other employment laws. Questions often arise about whether a person is serving the nonprofit as an employee, independent contractor, or a volunteer.

10. Properly address conflicts of interest involving directors and officers.

    Managing conflicts of interest does not mean prohibiting all that arise. Conflicts can be dealt with using a good policy statement that requires approval of the conflict by independent board members, recusal of the interested officer or director, and making sure the nonprofit receives fair market value.

11. Avoid unrelated business activities.

According to the IRS, for most organizations an activity is an unrelated business (and subject to unrelated business income tax) if it meets three requirements: *it is a trade of business, it is regularly carried on, and it is not substantially related to furthering the exempt purpose of the organization.* **Get good legal advice** for your nonprofit if you have unrelated business activity concerns, because the tax consequences for violating IRS standards are serious.

#3 Risk Management Planning

"If you don't invest in risk management, it doesn't matter what business you're in—it's a risky business."

— Gary Cohn

"You don't know who is swimming naked till the tide goes out."

— Warren Buffet

Nonprofit leaders and board members face an important decision in how to manage the various kinds of risks associated with operating a nonprofit. Nonprofits usually purchase insurance for obvious and common risks such as premises liability insurance, hazard insurance, and director and officer activity. This is prudent, but falls short of developing an actual risk management plan providing comprehensive planning and protection against mistakes and malfeasance.

Think of the threat this way. You know rain is in the forecast and that you have an umbrella in the closet. It could be a problem if that umbrella has Elmo from *Sesame Street* on it and is light enough for a child to carry. It might keep you a little bit dry in a downpour, but mainly not.

STEP 12: KEEP UP WITH CYBERSECURITY, REGULATORY COMPLIANCE, AND RISK MANAGEMENT

This section will teach you to assess and plan for that rainy day and make sure you're ready for what might reasonably come along. The consequences for not preparing, while rarer, can be catastrophic. The goal of any plan is to *avoid, reduce, prevent, budget for, or transfer* known risks.

Here are some common internal risks nonprofits face: unemployment claims, work-related injuries, financial malfeasance, product liability, sexual harassment claims, employee error, and human relations conflict. Some common external risks nonprofits face include: changes in government regulations, unanticipated political events, changes in the economy, lawsuits, and more recently, challenges to cyber security. Of course, there are additional risks that arise with the specific services offered by the nonprofit.

Here are some suggestions for how to begin developing a risk management plan. First, perform a risk assessment. What might occur during the daily operations of your nonprofit programs and services that could result in an injury to an employee, volunteer, client, or the public? What is the probable cost or loss to the organization's reputation and finances as a result of these identified events? Could that loss involve a temporary or even permanent shutting of your doors because of the resulting financial costs? Does your nonprofit have the necessary financial resources if the organization is sued?

This assessment will lead to a discussion about how the nonprofit can address the identified risks. Initially, nonprofit leaders should seek to mitigate risk factors through internal policies and procedures. As is often said, an ounce of prevention is worth a pound of cure.

Creating up-to-date policies and procedures that help nonprofit leaders and employees avoid mistakes that create liability are well worth the time investment. Risk avoidance is one main reason why nonprofits develop informative and clear employee handbooks, safety manuals, and training programs. Sometimes this work is dry as toast, but it's important to do it anyway.

Avoid fraud, embezzlement, and mistakes through strict financial policies that follow standard accounting procedures and create appropriate financial controls. Avoid getting sued by establishing a clear code of ethics and behavioral guidelines. Many claims against organizations are related either to financial or behavioral misconduct. While policies cannot prevent people from intentionally acting badly, they can sometimes prevent stupid behavior.

Consider the cautionary tale of Rita Crundwell. Rita is currently serving 19 years for the embezzlement of $53.7 million dollars from the city of Dixon, Illinois, where she worked as the appointed controller and treasurer from 1983 to 2012. Because of poor risk management planning and monitoring, Rita supported her extensive American Quarter Horse breeding operation with public funds. She conducted the largest municipal fraud in U.S. history! Despite suspicious signs and questions from officials from neighboring towns, city management and bank officials never carefully reviewed her activities.

STEP 12: KEEP UP WITH CYBERSECURITY, REGULATORY COMPLIANCE, AND RISK MANAGEMENT

Part of deciding what to do about the identified risks includes making decisions about what risks will be handled by the organization itself and what will be transferred to an insurance company. Most nonprofits opt for a combination of these two approaches. Keep in mind that risk retention is more hazardous for the nonprofit than sharing the risk with another party through a contract. Normally this decision is heavily influenced by how financially secure the nonprofit is. If a nonprofit has many assets, it may choose to risk share, but with a higher deductible to reduce the insurance premium. The key is to understand the nonprofit's risk appetite.

Once you know the potential risks and have assessed the cost in terms of reputation and finances, the next step is to build a risk management plan. Helpful tools for organizing the risk management discussion can easily be found online. One source, Capterra.com, provides information about risk management tools for free and for purchase. Look for one geared toward the services offered by your nonprofit.[86]

A good risk management plan only works if someone is responsible for monitoring, implementing, or adjusting it to change. Who is accountable for these functions is not always the same person or team, so make sure there is clear communication about who is responsible for each part of the plan.

Beyond that, the leadership team should spend time evaluating the plan yearly in terms of goals, new initiatives, or program growth. One thing is certain: as the nonprofit changes, so do the risks of operation. It's also helpful to connect with legal and accounting professionals in your area that send out periodic newsletters with industry updates and case studies. Whatever it takes to remind you to keep an eye on risk will help avoid nasty surprises and costs.

Well done! You are now more aware and better prepared to position your nonprofit for long-term, sustainable success. Your investment in learning how to enhance and protect your mission will serve you and those you lead well.

Now is also the time, when the pathways to sustainability are fresh in your mind to list them in order of priority. That exercise and others that accompany each chapter of the book can be found in a FREE companion workbook to *The Nonprofit Playbook* on my website: www.ElizabethMaring.com as my gift to you. Both books are great tools to use as discussion guides with your team, your board, for new board member orientation, or as a yearly check-in list on your bookshelf.

I hope this book, the free workbook and other resources on my website help to make your nonprofit a sustainable success.

My best wishes to you on your nonprofit quest to make your neighborhood, community and the world a better place.

INITIAL IMPACT OF THE PANDEMIC ON NONPROFITS

> *"This is exactly what we were trained to do.*
> *When it gets tough, you gotta get going."*
>
> — Dr. Alex Ulfers, a Cedar Falls native
> working at a hospital in Queens, N.Y.,
> considered the epicenter of the coronavirus
> outbreak in the United Statesohn C. Maxwell

Just before this book was completed, the world was plunged into a global health crisis. For public health reasons, the government mandated that both for profit and nonprofit businesses alter their operations for a time to quell the spread of the virus. Everything else about daily life changed, too. Zoom meetings became the norm for work, church services, and college classes. People argued about whether to wear a mask. Social unrest over race relations spiked. The long-term economic consequences of the pandemic are at this time unknown and will unfold for years to come.

A few things can be said now about nonprofit sustainability, however, even in the first wave of the world's response.

1. **Never have essential nonprofits been more important.** The world has been reminded of the essential nature of hospitals, food banks, food production pipelines, and other organizations that provide for the basic needs of vulnerable citizens. It has also been reminded of the need for arguably the biggest nonprofits, national, and state governments, to be prepared and ready for the totally unexpected. The collective frustration over the lack of available personal protective equipment, testing, ventilators, and an overall game plan will not soon be forgotten.

2. **All nonprofit leaders have had to swing their attention to things completely off their radar six months ago.** It is unprecedented that all nonprofit leaders would be focusing on how to receive and spend relief loans and other emergency funding. This has created a flood of helpful collaborative forums for information sharing. Innovation is happening at record speed. Nonprofit boards are more active and engaged than ever before.

3. **Nonprofits are mainly succeeding** at meeting the challenge of delivering their services in novel ways, but have experienced a significant uptick in costs to do so. This has

profoundly highlighted the need for nonprofits to maintain a rainy day fund—or, in this case, a tsunami fund.

4. **The strengths and weaknesses of each nonprofit prior to the pandemic are amplified by the pandemic—for good or for ill.** As a result, it is safe to say that many nonprofits will survive and thrive due to their preparedness but others, like those for-profit businesses that were on the edge, will find the pandemic hard to survive.

5. **The pandemic is validating the premise of this book:** that sustainable success depends on *consistently and effectively* maintaining organizational health, so that when the hard times hit, a nonprofit has what it takes to survive until the next sunny day. Nonprofits that have a good crisis management plan in place, sufficient rainy-day funds, ample volunteers, competent boards, ethical leaders—you get the idea—have a far better shot at being around after a crisis.

Acknowledgements

This book would not have been possible without the influence of my parents, Betty and Bill Vogelzang, who instilled in me the value of higher learning and service above self. They lived lives of commitment to family, church, community and country.

Clarence Maring, my husband, who has never tired in his support and encouragement of my personal and professional endeavors. He adds a layer of critical thinking and discernment to all of our discussions that have greatly enriched my life and the content and quality of this book.

Drs. Daniel and Alexandra Maring and Steven and Katherine Maring, our sons and their amazing spouses, who are already building their own legacies of service to hospitals, churches, and nonprofit boards.

Shavonne Clarke, my editor, whose exceptional skills have made my books better.

Carl Erickson, Janice Troeger, and Dr. Jeffrey Hoogstra, my experienced and savvy beta readers, who spent countless hours reading every word of the manuscript. Your honest, insightful, kind, and helpful feedback was so important to this work.

The many talented and high-integrity nonprofit leaders that have invited me in and mentored me on the nonprofit journey. I am profoundly grateful for each of you.

The wonderful and hardworking volunteers I have met along the way, most notably at Community Threads, who have embodied the epitome of selfless service.

Jesus, whose mission to redeem the world opened the door for me to serve him and others with gratitude, passion, and joy.

AN INVITATION

THANK YOU FOR READING MY BOOK

I appreciate all of your feedback, and
I love hearing what you have to say.

I need your input to make the next version
of this book and my future books better.

Please leave me a helpful review on Amazon
letting me know what you thought of the book.

Thanks so much!

—Elizabeth Maring

Do you want Elizabeth to come and speak to your
organization? Do you need individual or group coaching?
Contact her at: ElizabethMaring.author@gmail.com.

About the Author

ELIZABETH MARING has been an attorney since 1985 representing businesses and nonprofits. Throughout her career she has held staff leadership and board positions in numerous nonprofits including Azusa Pacific University, Willow Creek Community Church, Heartland Community Church, The Christian Leadership Alliance, Sharefest, Inc. and Community Threads. In 2011 she founded Community Threads, a Christian nonprofit social enterprise which generated over three million dollars in financial grants to benefit homeless women and children and provide educational scholarships to students in need. She lives in Michigan with her husband of 35 years, Clarence, and is the mother of two married sons, Daniel and Steven.

ENDNOTES

[1] America's Nonprofits: National Council of Nonprofits. (n.d.). Retrieved from https://www.councilofnonprofits.org/americas-nonprofits

[2] McKeever, B. (2019, March 1). The Nonprofit Sector in Brief. Retrieved from https://nccs.urban.org/project/nonprofit-sector-brief

[3] Not its real name.

[4] Pagnoni, L. A. (2018, September 25). Board Giving: The Most Recent Stats. Retrieved from https://lapafundraising.com/board-giving-recent-stats/

[5] Emmerson, S. (2019, March 21). Great Examples of Multiplatform Storytelling. Retrieved from https://www.echostories.com/great-examples-multiplatform-storytelling/

[6] Zelmer, T. (2020, February 3). A Guide to Donor-Advised Funds. Retrieved from https://www.philanthropy.com/specialreport/a-guide-to-donor-advised-funds/227

[7] Allyn, B. (2019, May 21). Top Reason For CEO Departures Among Largest Companies Is Now Misconduct, Study Finds. Retrieved from https://www.npr.org/2019/05/20/725108825/ top-reason-for-ceo-departures-among-largest-companies-is-now-misconduct-study-fi?utm_campaign=economy&utm_medium=RSS

[8] Pontefract, D. (2018, June 4). Millennials And Gen Z Have Lost Trust And Loyalty With Business. Retrieved from https://www.forbes.com/sites/danpontefract/2018/06/03/millen nials-and-gen-z-have-lost-trust-and-loyalty-with-business/ #2bee26576145

[9] Best Performance Appraisal Software: 2020 Reviews of the Most Popular Tools & Systems. (n.d.). Retrieved from https://www.capterra.com/performance-appraisal-software/

[10] Gallup, Inc. (2020, April 27). CliftonStrengths Online-Talentbewertung. Retrieved from https://www.gallup.de/ 182696/clifton-strengthsfinder.aspx

[11] The Enneagram Institute. (n.d.). Retrieved from https://www.enneagraminstitute.com/

[12] Jossey-Bass. (2012). *The nonprofit board answer book: a practical guide for board members and chief executives.* San Francisco.

[13] Chamorro-Premuzic, T., Murphy, C., Sehgal, K., Claman, P., & Knight, R. (2017, June 15). When Leaders Are Hired for Talent but Fired for Not Fitting In. Retrieved from https://hbr.org/2017/ 06/when-leaders-are-hired-for-talent-but-fired-for-not-fitting-in

[14] Chamorro-Premuzic, T., Murphy, C., Sehgal, K., Claman, P., & Knight, R. (2017, June 15). When Leaders Are Hired for Talent but Fired for Not Fitting In. Retrieved from https://hbr.org/2017/06/when-leaders-are-hired-for-talent-but-fired-for-not-fitting-in

[15] Norman Schwarzkopf Quotes. (n.d.). Retrieved from https://www.brainyquote.com/quotes/norman_schwarzkopf_163145

[16] Scazzero, P. (2015). *The emotionally healthy leader: how transforming your inner life will deeply transform your church, team, and the world.* Grand Rapids, MI: Zondervan.

[17] McKee, A., & Shapiro, M. (2015, August 12). The Emotional Impulses That Poison Healthy Teams. Retrieved from https://hbr.org/2015/07/the-emotional-impulses-that-poison-healthy-teams

[18] (2012, December 5). Retrieved from http://blog.corporatetrainingmaterials.com/tag/influence/

[19] Guerrero, D., Shaw, K., McCarthy, P., Auvin, J., Wishnick, A., Monson-Rosen, M., ... Nonprofits Insurance Alliance Group. (2020, April 1). Women In Nonprofit Leadership: Is There a Gender Gap? Retrieved from https://www.missionbox.com/article/127/women-in-nonprofit-leadership-is-there-a-gender-gap#

[20] Johnson, S. (2018, September 8). Sonia Johnson, Author at Society For Employee Relations. Retrieved from https://societyforemployeerelations.com/author/soniajohnson/

21 Johnson, S. (2018, September 8). Sonia Johnson, Author at Society For Employee Relations. Retrieved from https://societyforemployeerelations.com/author/soniajohnson/

22 Gunn, R. (n.d.). Alternative Dispute Resolution In A Work Setting. Retrieved from https://www.mediate.com/articles/gunn.cfm

23 DiSC Personality Test – Resources Unlimited: Human Resources Training & Consulting. (n.d.). Retrieved from https://resourcesunlimited.com/disc-personality-test/

24 Johnson, S., & Jensen, C. (2003). *Who moved my cheese?: for kids: an a-mazing way to change and win!* New York: G.P. Putnams Sons.

25 Economy, P. (2015, November 9). Help Your Employees Cope With Big Changes. Retrieved from https://www.inc.com/peter-economy/resolved-you-will-help-yur-employees-deal-with-change-in-2014.html

26 Lipman, V. (2018, December 3). How To Manage Generational Differences In The Workplace. Retrieved from https://www.forbes.com/sites/victorlipman/2017/01/25/how-to-manage-generational-differences-in-the-workplace/#34c5fd014cc4

27 The Advantages And Disadvantages Of ADR. (2017, November 26). Retrieved from https://albrightstoddard.com/advantages-disadvantages-adr/

[28] Eckfeldt, B. (2015, May 21). What rowing taught me about high-performance teams. Retrieved from https://www.businessinsider.com/what-rowing-taught-me-about-high-performance-teams-2015-5

[29] Coleman, J. (2017, November 28). Six Components of a Great Corporate Culture. Retrieved from https://hbr.org/2013/05/six-components-of-culture

[30] Greer, P. (2015). *Mission drift: the unspoken crisis facing leaders, charities, and churches.* Minneapolis, MN: Bethany House.

[31] The Salvation Army. (2020, May 25). Retrieved from https://en.wikipedia.org/wiki/The_Salvation_Army

[32] Collins, J. (2001). *Good to great: why some companies make the leap ... and others dont.* London: Random House.

[33] Starr, B., & Browne, R. (2019, August 23). Navy SEAL commander: We have 'drifted from our Navy core values'. Retrieved from https://www.cnn.com/2019/08/23/politics/navy-seal-commander-core-values/index.html

[34] The Four Lenses Strategic Framework. (n.d.). Retrieved from http://www.4lenses.org/setypology/mission_drift

[35] The Leading Mission-Aligned Investing Peer Learning Network for Endowments. (n.d.). Retrieved from https://www.intentionalendowments.org/about_ien

[36] Economy, P. (2019, January 15). The (Millennial) Workplace of the Future Is Almost Here – These 3 Things Are About to Change Big Time. Retrieved from https://www.inc.com/peter-economy/the-millennial-workplace-of-future-is-almost-here-these-3-things-are-about-to-change-big-time.html

[37] Strauss, K. (2017, September 27). The 10 Best Nonprofits To Work For In 2017. Retrieved from https://www.forbes.com/sites/karstenstrauss/2017/09/27/the-10-best-nonprofits-to-work-for-in-2017/#3f0724fa100c

[38] Maggie Overfelt, special to C. N. B. C. (2017, May 31). The new generation of employees would take less pay for these job perks. Retrieved from https://www.cnbc.com/2017/05/30/job-perks-prodding-millennials-to-work-for-less.html

[39] Post, J. (2019, October 1). Why a Positive Attitude in the Workplace Matters. Retrieved from https://www.businessnewsdaily.com/6912-develop-positive-mindset.html

[40] New study finds discrimination against women and racial minorities in hiring in the sciences. (n.d.). Retrieved from https://www.insidehighered.com/news/2019/06/07/new-study-finds-discrimination-against-women-and-racial-minorities-hiring-sciences

[41] Qualities of a Good Employee: The Top 50 Signs To Look For. (2020, May 21). Retrieved from https://www.drinkcoffee.com/qualities-good-employee/

[42] Mattioli, D. (2019, November 20). Amazon Has Become America's CEO Factory. Retrieved from https://www.wsj.com/articles/amazon-is-americas-ceo-factory-11574263777

[43] Bill & Melinda Gates Foundation announce $450m to End Polio. (n.d.). Retrieved from https://rotary9500.org/Stories/bill-melinda-gates-foundation-announce-450m-to-end-polio

[44] Taylor, S. (1987, May 5). HIGH COURT RULES THAT ROTARY CLUBS MUST ADMIT WOMEN. Retrieved from https://www.nytimes.com/1987/05/05/us/high-court-rules-that-rotary-clubs-must-admit-women.html

[45] Haanaes, K. (n.d.). Knut Haanaes. Retrieved from https://www.ted.com/speakers/knut_haanaes

[46] Bill Gates Quotes. (n.d.). Retrieved from https://www.brainyquote.com/quotes/bill_gates_122131

[47] Breakthrough, & Press. (2020, April 17). East Garfield Park: Chicago, IL. Retrieved from https://www.breakthrough.org/

[48] Walton, S., & Huey, J. (1993). *Sam Walton: made in America: my story*. New York: Bantam Books.

[49] Peterson, H. (2014, December 16). Wal-Mart Founder: 'Most Everything I've Done I've Copied From Someone Else'. Retrieved from https://www.businessinsider.com/wal-mart-history-of-copying-rivals-2014-12

[50] Five Insights of Breakthrough Innovation. (2020, April 2). Retrieved from https://innovationmanagement.se/2019/06/06/five-insights-of-breakthrough-innovation/

[51] Clear, J. (2016, August 30). How Innovative Ideas Arise. Retrieved from https://www.entrepreneur.com/article/281471

[52] CharityWatch Hall of Shame: The Personalities Behind Charity Scandals. (n.d.). Retrieved from https://www.charitywatch.org/charity-donating-articles/charitywatch-hall-of-shame

[53] UPDATE : United Way Tries to Portray United Front : A year after scandal racked the nation's largest philanthropic group, it is still grappling with local defections and a marked drop in fund raising. (1993, April 13). Retrieved from https://www.latimes.com/archives/la-xpm-1993-04-13-mn-22399-story.html

[54] Levy, M., Rubinkam, M., & Associated Press. (2017, June 2). 3 ex-Penn State officials sent to jail in Sandusky scandal. Retrieved from https://www.startribune.com/ex-penn-state-officials-face-sentencing-in-sandusky-scandal/425851713/

[55] Bob Ferguson. (2019, August 1). Retrieved from https://hawksbillgroup.com/bob-ferguson/

[56] Community Threads. (n.d.). Retrieved from https://communitythreads.org/

[57] Volunteering in U.S. Hits Record High; Worth $167 Billion. (2018, November 13). Retrieved from https://www.nationalservice.gov/newsroom/press-releases/2018/volunteering-us-hits-record-high-worth-167-billion

ENDNOTES

[58] Volunteer Training Tips: 4 Easy to Implement Strategies. (2017, December 18). Retrieved from https://www.volunteerhub.com/ blog/volunteer-training-tips/

[59] We set the standards in volunteermanagement software. (n.d.). Retrieved from https://www.volgistics.com/

[60] Empowering Boards & Inspiring Leadership. (n.d.). Retrieved from https://boardsource.org/

[61] CEO Succession Planning – Avoid Transition Trauma at Your Nonprofit. (2020, May 18). Retrieved from https://nonprofitrisk.org/resources/articles/ceo-succession-planning/

[62] Adams, T. H. (2010). *The nonprofit leadership transition and development guide: proven paths for leaders and organizations.* San Francisco: Jossey-Bass.

[63] Adams, T. H. (2010). *The nonprofit leadership transition and development guide: proven paths for leaders and organizations.* San Francisco: Jossey-Bass.

[64] McCambridge, R., McCambridge, R., Dubb, S., Dubb, S., Rubin, E., Rubin, E., ... Gilmore, T. (2016, May 17). The Importance of Linking Leadership Succession, Strategy, and Governance. Retrieved from https://nonprofitquarterly.org/the-importance-of-linking-leadership-succession-strategy-and-governance/

[65] Succession Planning for Nonprofits – Managing Leadership Transitions. (2020, March 18). Retrieved from https://www.councilofnonprofits.org/tools-resources/succession-planning-nonprofits-managing-leadership-transitions

[66] Succession Planning for Nonprofits – Managing Leadership Transitions. (2020, March 18). Retrieved from https://www.councilofnonprofits.org/tools-resources/succession-planning-nonprofits-managing-leadership-transitions

[67] Price, N., & Price, N. (2019, January 4). CEO/Board: Succession Planning for Nonprofit Organizations. Retrieved from https://www.boardeffect.com/blog/executive-directorceo-succession-planning-for-nonprofit-organizations/

[68] The Leadership in Leaving. (n.d.). Retrieved from https://buildingmovement.org/tools/the-leadership-in-leaving/

[69] (n.d.). Retrieved from https://philanthropyjournal.org/

[70] Trump, D. J. (2017, December). NSS BookLayout FIN 121917. Retrieved from https://www.afrc.af.mil/Portals/87/documents/PDC/National%20Security%20Strategy.pdf?ver=2020-03-10-102640-487

[71] Masaoka, J., & Wolfred, T. (2019, October 14). Succession Planning for Nonprofits of All Sizes. Retrieved from https://blueavocado.org/leadership-and-management/succession-planning-for-nonprofits-of-all-sizes/?highlight=Succession

[72] Price, N. (2019, January 04). CEO/Board: Succession Planning for Nonprofit Organizations. Retrieved from https://www.boardeffect.com/blog/executive-directorceo-succession-planning-for-nonprofit-organizations/

[73] Herman, M. L., & Gloeckner, E. (2020, May 18). CEO Succession Planning – Avoid Transition Trauma at Your Nonprofit. Retrieved from https://nonprofitrisk.org/resources/articles/ceo-succession-planning/

[74] Herman, M. L., & Gloeckner, E. (2020, May 18). CEO Succession Planning – Avoid Transition Trauma at Your Nonprofit. Retrieved from https://nonprofitrisk.org/resources/articles/ceo-succession-planning/

[75] Brook, C. (2018, December 04). What is the NIST Cybersecurity Framework? Retrieved from https://digitalguardian.com/blog/what-nist-cybersecurity-framework

[76] Ropeik, A. (2017, May 20). Small Indiana Nonprofit Falls Victim To Ransom Cyberattack. Retrieved from https://www.npr.org/2017/05/20/529257365/small-indiana-nonprofit-falls-victim-to-ransom-cyberattack

[77] Ropeik, A. (2017, May 20). Small Indiana Nonprofit Falls Victim To Ransom Cyberattack. Retrieved from https://www.npr.org/2017/05/20/529257365/small-indiana-nonprofit-falls-victim-to-ransom-cyberattack

[78] Carson, J. (2020, January 28). Cybersecurity for Dummies Free Download: Cyber Security Books PDF. Retrieved from https://thycotic.com/resources/wileys-dummies-cybersecurity/?utm_expid=.SZu1hR9SR7q4dw6O3YQRUA.0

[79] Cybersecurity Framework. (2020, May 21). Retrieved from https://www.nist.gov/cyberframework

[80] Vigliarolo, B. (2017, May 19). NIST Cybersecurity Framework: A cheat sheet for professionals. Retrieved from https://www.techrepublic.com/article/nist-cybersecurity-framework-the-smart-persons-guide/

[81] Segal, C. (n.d.). Chelsea Segal. Retrieved https://www.coxblue.com/6-simple-tips-to-increase-your-small-business-security-using-inexpensive-cybersecurity-measures/

[82] Koegler, S. (n.d.). 5 ways Employees Can Combat Cyber Threats & Data Breaches. Retrieved from https://www.business.att.com/learn/tech-advice/5-easy-ways-to-improve-your-cybersecurity.html

[83] Dwyer, K. (2019, April 15). 7 Critical Risks Facing Nonprofit Organizations. Retrieved from https://riskandinsurance.com/7-critical-risks-facing-nonprofit-organizations/

[84] Where to Find Nonprofit Financial Information. (n.d.). Retrieved from https://www.bridgespan.org/insights/library/philanthropy/where-to-find-nonprofit-financial-information

[85] Employer ID Numbers (EINs). (n.d.). Retrieved from https://www.nonprofitexpert.com/nonprofit-irs-topic-index/employer-id-numbers-eins/

[86] I just used Capterra to find software! (n.d.). Retrieved from https://www.capterra.com/

Made in the USA
Monee, IL
01 March 2023

28959624R00135